The Final Beat
Gardaí Killed in the Line of Duty

D1535581

The Final Beat

Gardaí Killed in the Line of Duty

Liz Walsh

Gill & Macmillan

Gill & Macmillan Ltd
Hume Avenue, Park West
Dublin 12
with associated companies throughout the world
www.gillmacmillan.ie
0 7171 3278 1
© Liz Walsh 2001
Design by Carole Lynch
Print origination by O'K Graphic Design, Dublin
Printed by Omnia Books Limited, Glasgow

This book is typeset in Goudy 10.5pt/14.5pt.

*The paper used in this book comes from the wood pulp of managed forests. For
every tree felled, at least one is planted, thereby renewing natural resources.*

All rights reserved.
No part of this publication may be copied, reproduced or transmitted in
any form or by any means, without permission of the publishers.

A CIP catalogue record for this book is available from the British Library.

1 3 5 4 2

For my mum, Pauline, and for Martin, my soul-mate

O ver the years, since 1972, I felt that the tragedy that befell us allowed us to appreciate all the more the agony endured by the families of the other policemen who died in the line of duty, north and south of the border. Most, if not all, were younger than my father had been and had left young children. We were relatively lucky in this respect in that only one of our family was under the age of twenty-one. We suffered a great loss; it affected us deeply and it still does. In my mother's case, at ninety years of age, a day does not pass without some mention of my father and what might have been. She was sixty-one at the time and it seems as if a lifetime has passed since. For myself, I feel that you never really get over an experience like this; time just allows you to come to terms with it, despite its awful brutality and its suddenness. It was senseless: what cause could be served by it? Nothing could possibly justify it. You try to accept it, eventually, and then you do the best you can to get on with life.

John Donegan, June 2001

Contents

Acknowledgments

The families of some of the gardaí that feature in this book very kindly agreed to be interviewed. I owe a huge debt of gratitude to the families of Richard Fallon, Samuel Donegan, Michael Clerkin, John Morley, Patrick Reynolds, Patrick McLaughlin and Jerry McCabe. Thanks too to the family of Gary Sheehan for supplying photographs and to Rosemary Reid. I owe a big thank you to the serving gardaí from all ranks who helped out in so many ways, but who for obvious reasons would not appreciate an individual mention here. You know who you are. Thanks too to those republicans and others who, by the nature of their involvement, must also remain anonymous. Thanks to retired gardaí Mick Egan, Jim Cannon, Patrick O'Brien and Paddy Egan for your help in 'looking back', to Garda Denis Connolly and to all those gardaí who helped to put me in touch with the individual families. I would also like to thank Superintendent John Farrelly and the team at the Garda Press Office for handling many of my queries during the course of my research. A big thank you is due to Diarmaid MacDermott of Ireland International for the use of his court files. Thanks also to

Frank McNally of *The Irish Times* and writer Evelyn Conlon for sharing with me their personal memories of two of the murdered gardaí, and to Aiden Boyle for helping out with photographs.

I would like to thank Rita O'Reilly and Emma Counihan for their support and friendship and all those other journalists who offered help and encouragement. Thanks to my mum, Pauline, for her endless support and to Martin for his love and support. Gratitude is also due to Jonathan Williams, and to my fellow law students for ensuring I was kept up to speed, particularly Rita and Jenny. My deepest gratitude is due to Ben O'Sullivan, who generously endured a long interview on a subject that I know was very painful. Thank you Ben.

Prologue

❧❧❧

On the morning of 16 October 1971, a man left his home on Dublin's north side and headed towards the nearest phone box, about a half-mile walk. He was a prominent member of Saor Éire, a republican splinter group active in the late 1960s and early 70s.

He was keeping a low profile. On 3 April 1970, Saor Éire members had shot dead Garda Richard Fallon during a bank robbery on Dublin's Arran Quay. The IRA had split and all eyes were on the North. The Fallon murder was proof that the Northern conflict, which had erupted the previous year, was spilling over into the Republic. However, as a member of Saor Éire, he had been under police surveillance.

The man had stopped using his own phone, but he made one serious blunder that morning. He used the nearest public phone available. It was tapped. As he was talking, Special Branch detectives in Dublin Castle were listening in on the conversation. Special Branch Superintendent Pat Doocey rang Detective Garda Mick Egan, telling him to report to the Castle at twelve o'clock. 'There's a big search on,' said Doocey. The

Branch were planning to raid a house in Baldoyle on the north side of Dublin that evening.

The rented house on Bayside Boulevard North was used by Saor Éire as a safe house. Some of the men named publicly as suspects in the Fallon murder were hiding out there, but they were to be moved to a different location that night. By early evening the police were ready to move.

It was dark when the Special Branch cars began pulling into Bayside Boulevard North, a cluster of three-bedroom semis. Doocey and his team jumped out and ran around to the back of the house. Detective Superintendent Ned O'Dea and a couple of other officers jumped the five-foot garden wall at the back. The other detectives pulled out their firearms and surrounded the front of the house. O'Dea burst open the sitting-room door and landed on top of a man who was sitting in an armchair watching wrestling on television. He was Patrick Dillon, one of seven men named publicly by the gardaí in connection with the Fallon murder. Dillon had no chance to react. He was overpowered and bundled upstairs. The operation was all over in seconds.

Mick Egan was out front with another detective garda, Tom Gavin, when they spotted a dark grey Triumph Herald driving into Bayside Boulevard North at about 20 miles per hour. It drew up opposite number 8, slowed down and turned. Gavin recognised the driver of the car. He was Joe Dillon, another of the suspects in the Fallon murder. Egan and Gavin hopped into one of the Branch cars — a new Mark 4 Ford Cortina — and pulled it across Dillon's path. Dillon put his foot to the floor and headed straight for the Cortina but the Cortina pulled aside in the nick of time. Joe Dillon saw his chance. His car screeched out of Bayside Boulevard North, chased by the Cortina. The Triumph drove through Bayside Square and Bayside Boulevard

South, turned left and sped along Sutton Downs, swerving onto the coast road in the direction of Howth, with the Branch car close behind. The two cars gathered speed as they raced up alongside a high wall at the Christian Brothers school and onto Baldoyle Road. Several times, the Cortina tried to overtake the Triumph but Dillon swerved across the road into its path.

The cars were travelling at a ferocious speed when a bus in front pulled out into traffic. Dillon got through but the gap was narrowing. Mick Egan, who was driving the Branch car, made a split-second decision to go for it. He careered through the gap between the bus and another car, taking the chrome off the left side of the Cortina and slicing the wing mirror off the other side. The cars drew abreast at the old railway crossing on Baldoyle Road. Mick Egan spotted a gun cocked out of the rear window of Dillon's car. The fuses had blown in the Cortina's radio, leaving the two detectives unable to call for backup.

Tom Gavin opened up with his Thompson sub-machine-gun. Unlike the IRA, which forbade its members from deliberately targeting the Irish army or gardaí, Saor Éire would not surrender its guns if confronted by the Irish security forces. Gavin aimed sideways and shot at the right front tyre of Dillon's car as Egan tried to jam it into the kerb, alongside a high wall. The bonnet of the Triumph shot up with the force of the blast from the Thompson and the shots wrecked the block of the engine. They glanced off the back right tyre and it collapsed, leaving the car lopsided and in danger of turning over. Dillon tried to turn between a kerb and a lamppost. Some distance on, the Triumph mounted the footpath, careered around the corner onto Brookstone Road and stopped.

The chase was over. Joe Dillon's gun, a .38 pistol with a round up the breech, was in its holster when he got out with his hands up. Seán Morrissey was in the back seat, armed. He dropped his pistol onto the floor of the car.

The blasts from the Thompson were the first shots fired by the gardaí in the Northern Troubles that were to overshadow the entire island for the next three decades.

1

Garda Richard Fallon

At the British Small Arms factory in Birmingham in 1969, an assembly worker was proofing nine-millimetre Star semi-automatic pistols. The pistols were part of a regular consignment from the Star munitions factory in Spain and were being tested in the Birmingham factory. Proofing was a technical process that involved putting component parts of the firearm onto a metal plate, placing another metal instrument on top and testing for defects. Every weapon, when it left the armoury, was in perfect working order. Each consignment contained a number of pistols with faulty components, which if not detected would result in the gun misfiring. These rejects were put aside for drilling, a process that put the gun out of commission until the parts could be broken down. For every consignment of two hundred pistols there would be fifteen or sixteen rejects, perhaps less.

The proofer picked up a pistol and put it through the tests. It was perfect. He put it into a bin marked 'Rejects'. Towards the end of his shift he retrieved the pistol. When it was safe to do so, he put it into a bag for going home. It did not appear anywhere on the list of weapons logged and sent into the stores. When he got home he placed it into a larger carton, about twelve inches by twelve, sealed it and wrapped a colour code around it. It was now ready for transportation by plane to Dublin Airport. Thirty years ago, it was relatively easy to get metal objects onto an aeroplane: x-ray machines and metal detectors were to come later. The proofer was being paid for his trouble by Saor Éire, an outlawed republican group that was behind a spate of armed robberies in Ireland in the late 1960s. The payments were made through a notorious Dublin criminal who acted as go-between for Saor Éire and the armoury contacts for a certain cut.

When the plane landed at Dublin Airport, an airport worker went out to the hold. He had been told to watch out for a box with a certain colour code. He found what he was looking for, tipped it to one side and later put it into the boot of his car. A day or two after, he met a member of Saor Éire and handed him the carton, and the republican paid him. Inside the carton was the Star pistol, two clips and a cleaning rod. The republican brought the contents to one of Saor Éire's arms dumps and put them in with the store of arms. In that way, members of Saor Éire had been arming themselves for years. (Soar Éire was not actually set up until March 1969; it was founded by a number of former IRA men who, anticipating the IRA split into Provisional and Official wings in December 1969/January 1970, had begun arms smuggling.)

This particular gunrunning line worked perfectly until the contacts in Britain attempted to knock off a container full of ammunition. The British authorities caught them, and two men were sentenced to twenty years apiece. The gardaí knew that parcels of arms had been filtering through from Britain, although they had not known the precise process by which they were getting through. The secretary of the Department of Justice, Peter Berry, also knew and had informed the Taoiseach, Jack Lynch, months before the Arms Crisis of 1970.

Saor Éire had been running rings around the gardaí. At that time, the force was simply not equipped to confront a group of well-armed and highly motivated bank robbers. Between 1967 and 1969, eighteen banks in the South had been robbed, most of them by republicans who would form Saor Éire. The organisation had also carried out the largest bank robbery in the country, until then, when in March 1969 an eight-man gang had robbed two banks in Newry, County Down, simultaneously. The raids had been carried out with military precision, and the gang escaped with £22,000, a huge amount at the time. For a while after, the organisation was flush with cash. When funds began to dwindle, they would pull another bank job. It was only a matter of time before the inevitable happened.

GARDA RICHARD Fallon was on duty on 3 April 1970. A married man, and father of five young children, he was from Kilrooskey in County Roscommon. The forty-three-year-old garda was known to friends and family as Dick. He had joined the gardaí in 1947 and was stationed in Dublin for his entire career. At the time of his death he was attached to Mountjoy Garda Station. Because of an ulcer he worked regular hours, generally nine to five.

At around 10.40 a.m. on 3 April, three men walked up the steps of the Royal Bank of Ireland on Dublin's Arran Quay. One was wearing a green anorak with a hood pulled over his head; another wore a brown coat with a scarf around his neck and held a holdall in his left hand. The third man stood near the front of the bank. A railing separates the bank grounds from the footpath. Immediately to the right is a private passageway leading to the rear of the building with a gate at the end, leading to Stable Lane. The lane extends from Smithfield to Lincoln Lane, which runs northward from Arran Quay. That morning, a gold-coloured Ford Cortina parked at Lincoln Lane close to a telegraph pole. One of the telephone wires was cut.

Thirteen officials were on duty inside the bank: there were just four customers. The bank manager, Stanley Keegan, was on the telephone in his office when the call was cut off. When he checked with the switchboard, the operator told him the line had gone dead. Moments later, he heard a commotion in the main bank floor and heard a voice saying 'This is a stick-up.' A gunman was standing with his back to Keegan, shouting and waving a gun in the air from left to right. The manager sat there, momentarily frozen, and then went for the alarm button behind his chair. It too was out of action.

One cashier, Richard McCorduck, had been about to cash a customer's cheque at the time the gunmen entered the bank. He saw two of them pulling masks down over their faces. The first gunman jumped onto the counter. The second rushed forward and stood on the middle counter, shouting 'This is a raid, stand back.' A customer, Stephen Kennedy, had come into the bank just moments before the gunmen. Kennedy, a telephonist with the Department of Defence, had taken a couple of steps towards the cashier's desk when a voice to his right told him to move. When he turned around he saw a masked man holding what appeared to be a machine-gun. 'Get over there the rest of you,' the gunman said. He ordered the customers to face the wall: 'Stay where you are or you'll get this.' His two accomplices cleared out the loose money behind the counter, scooping the

4

cash into a bag with one hand while holding a gun in the other. One of them grabbed a black cash box from behind the counter before he vaulted back over the counter. 'Don't follow us or you'll have it,' warned one of the raiders as they made for the main door of the bank. They had £3,270 in the bag.

When the telephone wire had been cut it had registered as an alarm fault at Chubb Alarms. Chubb's technician, Thomas Rowan, rang the garda on duty at radio control at Dublin Castle, who alerted the Central Detective Unit. Radio control put out a message asking patrol cars in the area to check on the bank at Arran Quay. Three uniformed officers — Dick Fallon, Garda Paul Firth and Garda Patrick Hunter — were in the vicinity. Firth picked up the call and told control they were in a patrol car in North King Street, not far from Arran Quay. Turning to Fallon in the back seat, Hunter asked if he was getting out. Before the radio message had come through, Fallon had said something about having to make a phone call. 'No,' he replied, 'I will go along with you.' Hunter gunned the engine and drove into Smithfield, turning right when he got to Lincoln Lane. They drove passed the gold Cortina parked at the telegraph pole but noticed nothing out of the ordinary. They kept going, turning onto Arran Quay and pulling up outside the Royal Bank of Ireland, close to the kerb. Hunter called radio control and told the duty officer that they had arrived at the bank.

Firth walked around the back of the patrol car and followed Fallon through the gateway in front of the bank, just as the raiders were coming out. A tall, masked man held the door open from the inside to let the others out. An elderly man, John Cowle, was standing in the portico of the bank. The man holding the machine-gun pointed it at the old man and warned him to 'Stand back, stand back.' The three men rushed out in single file, went down the steps and were turning left when they saw the gardaí coming towards them. All three were armed: the gardaí, of course, were unarmed. They pointed their guns at the gardaí as Firth and Fallon began to close in on them. The three opened fire simultaneously, each of them firing at least two shots. Firth shouted at Hunter to call radio control for backup.

The gunmen were now standing at the entrance to the private passageway along the side of the bank. Fallon was within a few feet of the entrance with his right arm extended as though he was about to grab one of the armed men when a shot fired by a second gunman hit him. Garda Fallon fell face downwards onto his left side with blood pouring down the right side of his face. His garda cap was on the ground beside him.

People inside the bank had heard the sound of gunfire and came running out. Stanley Keegan saw two figures on the ground, Fallon and Firth. Garda Fallon was completely prostrate; Firth was lying slightly behind and across, having dived onto the ground when the shooting started. He shouted for someone to get an ambulance. Vincent Keogh, a passer-by, had been in Lincoln Lane when he heard the shots. He ran towards the bank and climbed on top of the railing to see what was going on. At the far end of the passageway he saw men that he thought looked familiar. Then he remembered seeing them some minutes earlier when they had parked the gold Cortina. The three raiders, one carrying a bag, ran towards the car, where another man had the engine running. It took off with a screech of tyres. Another passer-by, Martin Coleman, saw the car taking off and jotted down the number, which he later passed to the gardaí.

Dick Fallon was lying in the passageway unconscious. One of the first on the scene was Fr Joseph Drumgoole. He felt for a pulse but there was none. Two firemen arrived from Dorset

Street station at 10.58 and found no sign of life. They placed the garda on a stretcher and rushed him to casualty at nearby Jervis Street Hospital, where, a short time later, doctors pronounced him dead. The raid and the killing had taken less than six minutes. The fatal bullet had entered the back of Dick Fallon's neck on the left side, passed up through his neck, severing the spinal cord, and exited near his right ear. Another bullet, a .22, had entered the back of his left shoulder and travelled down his arm, shattering the bone. Dick Fallon had died almost instantly. The fatal shot had been fired from a nine-millimetre pistol.

DICK FALLON was the first member of the Garda Síochána to be murdered since 1942, when Garda George Mordant had been shot dead attempting to arrest a wanted man. The Fallon killing had a profound effect on a Southern public not yet inured to the violence that was engulfing Northern Ireland. On the day he was buried, Dublin came to a complete standstill. The government had not ordered a state funeral, yet one thousand uniformed gardaí turned up to line the route. The killing had caused some friction within the force, as rank-and-file gardaí felt that the armed section should have been sent to Arran Quay. Up until three weeks before the raid, gardaí had been placed on regular security duty outside city and suburban banks. Members of the force felt that those involved in such security should be armed. The request went to the government, which turned it down.

Garda Fallon's eldest son, Richard, remembers clearly the day his father was buried. At the time, he was eleven years old:

> All the way along the route all you could see was a sea of uniforms. Old people were kneeling saying the rosary by

the side of the road. It was still that kind of Dublin then, it was a very post Civil War scene really, very surreal. I remember we were driving up by O'Connell Street and looking up at the monument and seeing people right up on top of it, and on lampposts, like they do for the Patrick's Day Parade. Everyone assumes that my father was given a state funeral. He wasn't: it just looked like one because so many gardaí had turned out in force. My mother paid for my father's funeral herself.

Dick Fallon's family heard about his death around lunchtime on the day of the shooting. At the time, they lived at Lorcan Road on Dublin's north side:

> We had been off on a school break. The five of us were like steps of stairs; Finian, the youngest, was only three. I heard on the news . . . that a guard had been shot in Dublin. There was no name. The guards were searching cars around the area looking for the bank robbers; there were guards all over the place. My mother was sticking the dinner in the oven, around half one or two, when Fr Clarence [Daly], the garda chaplain, came up the path with a local GP. I knew then. I assumed it was my father and that he was dead.

The five children were then gathered up and ushered across the road to a neighbour's house, where they spent the afternoon. A garda was placed on duty outside the Fallon family home:

> We were brought that afternoon for a spin to the Coachman's Inn for a bottle of orange. When we got back home the GP brought us children into the sitting-room

and he said: 'Your Dad's gone to Heaven.' Most of us were too young to know what Heaven was. I remember they brought back my father's cap and his watch and gave them to my mother. The watchstrap was caked in blood where they hadn't cleaned it. I remember brushing the flakes of blood from it.

Looking back, Richard Fallon is quite cynical about the authorities' treatment of his family:

Of course there was no such thing as counselling. We subsequently found out that the first thing my mother was given was sedatives: she was on them for three years. It was only when she came off them that the grief hit her, and there she was, with five children hanging out of her. And that's the way we were left. She always felt that she had been 'handled' [by the authorities]. It was a complete circus around the funeral and then nothing, no backup, absolutely nothing.

After the funeral, Dick Fallon's widow, Deirdre, received a lot of hate mail, saying that her husband had acted stupidly in confronting the gunmen. Some accused the family of 'living off the state'. There were also references, in the letters and in the press, to the clothes she had worn to her husband's funeral. Mrs Fallon was 'instantly reminiscent' of Jacqueline Kennedy, according to an *Irish Press* reporter. 'My mother was very hurt by all of this,' Richard Fallon recalls.

IN OCTOBER 1969, six months before the Fallon murder, the garda authorities had printed the names, addresses and photographs of fifteen of their most wanted men in *Fógra Tóra*, a confidential garda document circulated to members of the force. After Garda Fallon's murder, senior gardaí wasted no time in running their eyes over this list. Within a few hours it was shortened to seven men, all members of Saor Éire. Three of the men named were Joseph Dillon, Seán Morrissey and Patrick Francis (Frank) Keane. The garda authorities printed seven thousand photos of these men and distributed them among gardaí of all ranks. They also took the unprecedented step of naming the seven men in the national media, asking them to report to the Bridewell Garda Station in Dublin. Two of the addresses supplied to the media by the gardaí were incorrect: one was that of *Irish Times* news editor Donal Foley.

Whatever about the individuals who may have been involved, there was no doubt that Saor Éire had been behind the bank robbery and the killing of Garda Fallon. The nine-millimetre murder weapon has never been found, but it is virtually certain that it was one of the Star nine-millimetre calibre pistols smuggled in from Britain. There appears to be some basis to the rumours that certain authorities within the state had allowed the weapons through for the purpose of tracing. Also, there is little doubt that an informer had been passing high-grade information to the authorities, and they were anxious that he should not be exposed, a fact referred to by the Taoiseach, Jack Lynch, after the murder.

The killing happened just before the Arms Crisis of 1970 exploded and at a time when Fianna Fáil was split down the middle over the North. 'The killing of Garda Fallon could not have come at a worse time,' recalls Belfast republican John Kelly, who was one of those charged and acquitted in the 1970 Arms Trial. 'Saor Éire was out of control, I don't know what they were at, but they certainly were not helping matters.' The government's offer of a £5,000 reward for information leading to the arrest of the killers was seen at the time as, at best, a shrewd political gesture and, at worst, a clumsy attempt at damage limitation. In the weeks and months after the killing, rumours abounded about connections between Saor Éire and certain members of the government, particularly Neil Blaney, who was Minister for Agriculture until his dismissal from the government by Jack Lynch in May 1970. One theory was that elements within the state had colluded with the outlawed organisation because of the Northern situation. Des O'Malley, who was Minister for Justice during this period, has confirmed that, while aware of the rumours, he never found anything to substantiate them.

None of the documentation that has come to light since has substantiated this theory, although it is clear that certain members of Fianna Fáil had connections with individual members of Saor Éire. Neil Blaney had been a friend of Liam Walsh, a member of Saor Éire who was blown to pieces while planting a bomb along the Heuston Station to Connolly Station railway line in 1970. The bomb was intended for the nearby army magazine fort. A second Saor Éire man, Martin Casey, was injured in the premature explosion.

In November 1969, Casey and a member of Fianna Fáil had travelled to London, allegedly to buy arms. When they were signing in at the Irish Club in London's Eaton Square, Casey gave a false name and the Fianna Fáil man gave the name of George Dixon. This, incidentally, was the name under which a bank account had been opened in Baggot Street in Dublin to hold some of the £100,000 voted by the Dáil for the relief of distress of Northern nationalists. The head of the Special Branch, Superintendent John Fleming, raised the arms-buying expedition during a Dáil Public Accounts Committee inquiry into related affairs in December 1970. Other inexplicable events were happening behind closed doors. In February 1970, the Central Detective Unit were on the point of rounding up known members of Saor Éire following a raid on the Hibernian Bank at Rathdrum, County Wicklow. At the last minute, someone in authority halted the round-up. The Rathdrum raid was the seventh Saor Éire raid in a two-year period. In a commando-like operation, seven men cut all the telephone lines into the village and stopped all traffic, including a car being driven by a uniformed garda. Having virtually taken over the village, the gang robbed the bank, and stole several cars along the escape route to replace the original getaway cars. It was just six weeks before Garda Fallon was shot dead at Arran Quay.

By that stage, Saor Éire had built up a stockpile of training equipment, arctic-type sleeping bags, army boots and flak jackets, as well as arms and ammunition. Its base was a rented cottage in a cul-de-sac off the Lackan to Valleymount road in County Wicklow. Saor Éire members used the heavy filling in the sleeping bags to hide some of the guns.

Some of the seven men named publicly by the gardaí in the wake of the Fallon murder were on the run for bank raids, including Joe Dillon. In July 1966, Dillon had been found guilty of a rent office robbery in north County Dublin and sentenced to five years in Mountjoy, reduced to three on appeal. On 18 August 1967, he was transferred by ministerial order to Portlaoise, but he challenged the transfer order in the High Court. The court upheld his appeal and the gardaí were forced to obtain fresh warrants relating to Portlaoise. They were gone from the court for just one hour, during which time Dillon was technically free. He went into the toilet of the Four Courts, put his hand up the cistern where a Walter pistol had earlier been planted and put it in his pocket. He then jumped the railings at the front of the Four Courts, collided with a garda on a bicycle, hopped into a waiting car and escaped.

Frank Keane, meanwhile, was protesting his innocence in the national media in the form of a letter he delivered to all the daily papers on 5 April, the day after the seven men were named as suspects:

> As one of the seven persons requested by the police to help with the investigations into the murder of Garda Fallon, I hereby make my reasons clear for not doing so.
>
> 1. I am a member of a political organisation, the rules of which forbid any collaboration with opposing forces.
> 2. As a person who was wrongfully accused (without any evidence whatsoever) of a bank robbery in Newbridge in June '68, and having subsequently received a *nolle prosequi* … I do not feel at all inclined to help the police with their inquiries, even if there was any assistance I could give.
> 3. As a person who was intimidated by the Special Branch into signing a statement admitting arson etc. at the Fianna Fáil HQ in October 1967, and subsequently received a six months prison sentence, I do not at all feel confident about getting fair play at the hands of the police.
> 4. As a person who has been harassed, insulted, assaulted and intimidated by the Special Branch on

many occasions, I can only say that the police have a 'hell of a neck' in asking me for any assistance.

While I am writing this letter on my own behalf, I think that it is only fair to point out that most of the people mentioned on the list have nothing whatsoever to gain by presenting themselves to the police for questioning, as there is a possibility that some at least could be detained for other offences. The police are very well aware of this fact and know that these people cannot come forward and clear themselves of this very serious insinuation without being detained for something else. One can only deplore this attempt by the police to make scapegoats out of the people who are in all possibility quite innocent of this unfortunate crime.

Frank Keane

PS I am putting my right thumbprint on the bottom of this page for authenticity. I am sure the police could help to have it verified if necessary.

Shortly after Keane's letter was reproduced on the front pages of the newspapers he went on the run. He fled to Britain, but after a protracted legal battle, which went all the way to the House of Lords, Keane was extradited back to Ireland to stand trial for the murder of Dick Fallon. The main plank of evidence against him was visual identification by Garda Paul Firth, who gave evidence that he had a full frontal view of Keane. Other witnesses testified that the gang had been fully masked throughout. The jury acquitted him. Keane walked out of court a free man, his innocence established. But from the moment he left the courthouse he was kept under constant garda surveillance.

THE ARREST of Joe Dillon and Seán Morrissey was one of the most dramatic ever made by the gardaí. Some of the wanted men had been hiding out at a Saor Éire safe house in Bayside Boulevard North on Dublin's north side. They were to be moved on the night of 16 October and the Special Branch wanted to get there first. Shortly after 10 p.m. the gardaí raided the house at Bayside Boulevard North and took Patrick Dillon into custody. However, he was subsequently released without charge. Joe Dillon and Seán Morrissey arrived in a grey Triumph car just as the raid was in progress. Spotting Dillon, who was driving, detective gardaí Mick Egan and Tom Gavin quickly pulled a Special Branch car across the road in an attempt to block him. Dillon put his foot to the floor, forcing the garda car to pull back at the last second. Joe Dillon was from north Dublin and knew the roads better than the gardaí. He zigzagged through a maze of narrow streets before swerving out onto the coast road to Howth, chased by the Special Branch car.

'Dillon knew the country well,' recalls Mick Egan, who has since retired. 'We were driving up by a high wall outside church grounds and I said to Tom "We'll try and nudge them into the kerb." Our car radio had gone down with the ferocity of the chase; the fuses had blown, so we couldn't call for backup. They had a gun at the window and Tom opened up with his Thompson and fired at the wheel. With the force of the blast the bonnet of their car shot up. Tom Gavin never took his pipe out of his mouth. I'll always remember that, at the end of it he was still smoking his pipe. We didn't know until we got out of the car that Seán Morrissey was in the car with Joe Dillon.'

Egan took Dillon's Walter pistol and holster from around his waist and removed a magazine from his jacket pocket. The detective then asked Morrissey where was his gun and he pointed to the floor of the car. That night was the first time that the gardaí had seen Joe Dillon since his escape from the Four Courts in 1967. The two men were taken to the Bridewell Garda Station and asked to account for their movements between 9 a.m. and noon on 3 April 1970. They refused to say anything. On 25 October, Dillon and seven other men took part in an identity parade at the Bridewell. None of the civilian witnesses was able to make a positive identification. The next into the room was Garda Paul Firth. He studied the line-up for a few minutes and then walked slowly from right to left. He then walked straight over to Joe Dillon and placed his hand on him.

'I saw this man coming out of the bank, the second man out of the bank, on the morning of 3 April. He opened fire on Garda Fallon and myself, killing Garda Fallon.'

'Are you familiar with my photograph?' Dillon asked Firth.

'I saw a photograph purporting to resemble Joseph Dillon.'

'Who am I?'

'Joseph Dillon,' Firth replied.

Garda Patrick Hunter, who was also at the bank that morning, was unable to identify anyone.

Three days later, Dillon and Morrissey were charged with the capital murder of Garda Richard Fallon and with possession of firearms with intent to endanger life.

THE TRIAL of Dillon and Morrissey opened in the Central Criminal Court sitting in the Green Street courthouse in January 1972. Like that of Frank Keane, it was held before a jury. (In December 1972 juries were abolished for trials involving subversive crimes and were replaced by the non-jury Special Criminal Court under the Offences Against the State

(Amendment) Act 1972.) Visual identification was to be crucial for a conviction. But in this case the state had one additional piece of evidence — the existence of Dillon's palm print and Morrissey's fingerprint on a copy of the *Evening Herald* allegedly found in the gold Cortina getaway car, which matched prints taken from the house in Lackan.

Almost immediately, the prosecution ran into difficulty with Garda Firth's evidence. Firth had testified that the doors of the Royal Bank had burst open from the inside. It was found that they opened inwards. Firth admitted the mistake. Cross-examined by defence counsel Seán MacBride, he then admitted that the mouths, nose and chins of the men had been masked and their heads covered. This, said MacBride, contradicted his evidence that he could see that one of the men had black hair. Garda Firth agreed with MacBride that within two or three days of the murder he had asked to see photographs of Saor Éire members on the wanted list. He also recalled seeing Dillon's and Morrissey's names in the papers.

'And you got the photographs of seven people?' MacBride asked.

'Seven or eight, whichever it was.'

'Including the photographs of the two accused?'

'That is right,' Firth agreed.

'Naturally, garda, you were outraged by this awful murder?'

'Yes.'

'And anxious to get someone for it?'

'To get the people concerned.'

MacBride said that Firth was in no way an untruthful witness, but suggested that his recall may have been affected by the shattering experience outside the bank on the morning of the killing and the death of his colleague.

On the fingerprint evidence the state's case became totally unstuck. The main fingerprint expert, Sergeant William Byrne, testified that he had found a twelve-point match of Dillon's palm print on the newspaper. The standard adopted by Scotland Yard was sixteen. Byrne was handed a magnifying glass and asked to count the ridges in the area he had marked on a Xerox copier. He said there were twenty-four or twenty-five. MacBride then went into the witness box with Byrne and the two counted them again, but did not agree on the number. Byrne was then asked if it was possible that the prints of one of his colleagues were on the newspaper. 'Not that I know of, but it is possible,' Byrne replied.

Directing the jury, Mr Justice Seamus Henchy said that although the case did not depend entirely on the fingerprint evidence, it was nonetheless of crucial importance. If the jury believed the prints belonged to Dillon and Morrissey, that would be a starting-point from which they could go on to consider other evidence. If, however, they could not agree on the prints, the accused would be entitled to an acquittal. The jury took seven hours to bring in a verdict. During that time, hundreds gathered outside the old stone courthouse in Green Street. Among them were seven internees who, days earlier, had escaped from the *Maidstone* prison ship moored off Belfast Lough. It was 12.20 a.m. on 17 January when the jury returned with an acquittal. Inside and outside the courthouse, supporters of the men burst into spontaneous applause. Their role over, the twelve jurors were left to walk home in the early hours of the morning. Neither Dillon nor Morrissey was released, as they still faced charges of possession of firearms on 16 October 1971, the day of their arrest. Both were later convicted and sentenced to eighteen months.

PAUL FIRTH died in 1991 while in his mid-forties, never having fully got over the killing of his colleague or the subsequent trials. Deirdre Fallon, a former nurse, died in 1994 at the age of fifty-seven. After their father's death, Richard Fallon had to become something of a surrogate father to the younger children:

> I knew enough to sense all the implications and became the kind of Daddy of the house. My teens were taken away from me. When my mother got upset there were periods when we'd have to fend for ourselves. She'd take Valium for the bouts of depression. We never felt anything for the men who killed our father apart from when things were really bad; then I'd say, 'Yeah, you guys really fucked us up.' On the funny side, when we were really getting on my mother's nerves she'd say 'Your father took the easy way out running up the lane that day.' She certainly didn't have it easy after my father died. That Christmas, our house at Lorcan Road burned down. We spent that Christmas on camp beds in my grandmother's house in Raheny.

Richard Fallon is now in his early forties and is a first secretary in the Department of Foreign Affairs:

> I remember being at a conference on children in conflict and talking to children from Bosnia and it was only then I realised that children who have lost a parent actually become parents themselves to the surviving spouse. We identified with each other. After my father's death I always identified with Northern Ireland. For every person killed there, there are thirty others whose lives have been tainted by it. I remember in 1997 watching an RUC funeral on the

TV and seeing his kids walking behind their father's coffin and saying to myself 'the cycle continues'. For the families, whether the victim was a guard, an RUC man or a republican, the grief is the same. And it's the same justification behind the killing. That line, the one that's often read at funerals — 'Greater love hath no man than this, that he lay down his life for his friends' — can apply anywhere, at any funeral. When I was a kid I used to think 'My Dad's on the right side and anyone on the other side has to be a baddy.' As I grew up and saw the suffering in the North, people having their civil rights denied, you realise things are a bit more complex than that, but, because of our family's experience, I became acutely aware of the futility of the armed option.

Despite their experience, the Fallon family are totally against capital punishment: 'We did not support it; neither did my mother. It might satisfy a need for revenge but it would simply create a new layer of problems. I feel it is the ultimate cop-out.'

Five years after Dillon and Morrissey's acquittal, disturbing evidence emerged which cast doubt on the way in which fingerprint evidence had been analysed in their case. It came to light when a print accidentally placed on a helmet by Detective Sergeant Michael Diggin of the garda fingerprint section was wrongly identified as belonging to a suspect in the 1976 murder of the British Ambassador, Christopher Ewart-Biggs, in Dublin. The same fingerprint-matching method had been used in the Dillon and Morrissey case. Diggin discovered the mistake and brought it to the attention of Detective Sergeant Patrick Corliss, who in turn alerted Sergeant William Byrne. Diggin and Corliss also brought their concerns to the attention of superior officers, all the way to the Commissioner, Edmund Garvey.

Nothing happened until the scandal broke in *The Irish Times* in February 1977. In March, the Deputy Commissioner, Patrick McLaughlin, sought the help of an outside expert, Commander G.T.C. Lambourne, head of the fingerprint section at Scotland Yard. Lambourne agreed with Diggin's assessment. The net effect was that the credibility of the fingerprint section was seriously undermined. Corliss then began trawling through cases in which William Byrne had been involved. He obtained photographic enlargements of the charts used in the Dillon and Morrissey case and concluded that the identification made by Byrne had been wrong. If the men had been convicted in 1972, there was a high probability that they would have hanged, given the public outcry over the killing. And it would have emerged years later that their convictions were unsafe.

THIRTY YEARS on, the Fallon family are pressing for the file on their father's killing to be reopened. The Department of Justice has so far steadfastly refused to release the Fallon files to the National Archives under the thirty-year rule. It is possible that there is no smoking gun surrounding the Fallon murder. All the available evidence points to a high degree of muddle in the handling of the investigation. But crucial questions remain. Why, when gardaí realised there was something wrong, were unarmed gardaí sent to the bank instead of the armed wing, which was based at Dublin Castle, a stone's throw from Arran Quay? Days after the murder, children picked up spent cartridges from the bullets near the grotto at Arran Quay. Why was the murder scene not properly sealed off? Why was the planned round-up of key members of Saor Éire after the Rathdrum raid halted at the last minute, and who gave the order? It may well be that back in 1970, the gardaí were simply not equipped to confront a well-armed and organised gang like Saor Éire. It may also be that the Department of Justice may be forced to admit that the authorities had not adequately investigated the fingerprint scandal, which may in turn expose certain miscarriages of justice. So long as the department refuses to address those questions, suspicions will remain.

Almost three decades after his acquittal, Joe Dillon says he supports the Fallon family's call for an inquiry into the killing of their father. 'The jury came to the right decision in our case. We have nothing to fear from an inquiry. We would welcome it and they should do it sooner rather than later. Or are they afraid that the fingerprint evidence used in our case might open up a whole new can of worms they would rather keep closed?'

2

Garda Inspector
Samuel Donegan

A silver-framed photograph of a smiling man in full garda uniform stands in pride of place in the living-room of Frances McGrath's south Dublin home. The snapshot, capturing a moment in time, is of her father, Inspector Samuel Donegan, who was killed in a booby-trap explosion along the border on 8 June 1972. Who killed him, no one knows. Why he was killed remains entirely speculative. No organisation has ever claimed responsibility for the bomb, and the joint Garda Síochána/RUC investigation has long since run into the sand.

Of all the gardaí killed during the three decades of the Troubles, Samuel Donegan — or Sam as his family knew him — seems to be the forgotten victim, remembered only by his family and friends. In contrast to the murders of other gardaí, the level of media coverage afforded to the Donegan killing was pitifully low. It occupied the front page for just a day, details were scant, follow-up reports were few and limited mainly to coverage of the funeral. No one was ever charged with his killing, so there was never a trial. It appears as though Sam Donegan's death happened almost in passing and with barely a mention. Only those who have been affected by this unexpected and violent intrusion into their lives remember. Sam Donegan's widow, Mary, is now ninety years old. Some details blur with the passage of time, others remain as clear as if they happened only yesterday. But nearly thirty years on, Sam Donegan's family are still wondering what happened on that day, because they were never told. Three decades later, they are pressing the garda authorities for some answers. To date, none has been forthcoming.

SAM DONEGAN was the first garda to be killed on duty in the border area during the Troubles. At sixty, he was also the oldest, approximately two years from retirement age. Stationed in Cavan town, he had four daughters — Maura, Frances, Kathleen and Sheila — two sons — John and Michael — and one grandchild, Louise. That day, 8 June, people on both sides of the border rose to a beautiful summer morning. Sam Donegan was due in court in Cavan at 10.30 a.m. When he had finished his court business he got a call from his superintendent, telling him that reports had come in of suspicious boxes on unapproved roads near the Cavan–Fermanagh border. First reports of the road bombs had been phoned into the garda station by early-morning motorists who had spotted two crates lying on the road. Not everyone saw them: an ambulance and several buses had driven past without stopping. Sam Donegan nipped home to Highfield Road to collect his wellington boots. His wife, Mary, was having tea with a neighbour. 'Is there a cup in that for me before I go?' the inspector asked his wife. He drank it standing beside the glass case in the living-room. 'Where's my wellingtons?' he asked, heading for the door. 'If I'm not back for my dinner I'll give you a ring.'

Sam Donegan's garda unit were accompanied by a military patrol as they headed for the unapproved roads off the main Cavan to Clones road. At that time, there was no army bomb disposal unit, although officers experienced in dismantling bombs were stationed at Athlone and Dublin. Among the military patrol was a young second lieutenant named John Gallagher. The joint patrol sealed off the area and began a search. It was just before midday when they came across the first box, a well-constructed wooden crate. It was lying on the road about one hundred yards on the Northern side of the border. A crude, hand-painted, wooden sign with large, white letters saying 'bomb' was standing five yards in front of the crate. Donegan noticed a cord leading from the box across a stream to the Southern side of the border. He tugged at the cord and toppled the box into a ditch. When the crate was opened it was empty. It was an obvious hoax.

The joint patrol then moved on to the second crate. It had been placed about two hundred and fifty yards away on Leggikelly Lane, Drumbonena, a lonely border road lined with trees and bushes just off the Redhills to Clones road. Sam Donegan was bending over it when it exploded. He took the full force of the bomb in the face. John Gallagher was standing beside him when the bomb went off. He suffered severe leg injuries. The bomb was made of gelignite, and it was thought that it was detonated from a nearby field. Army and garda patrols that later searched the area said there were no wires or cords running from the crate containing the bomb. In a follow-up search on the Northern side of the border, British troops found a 110-pound gelignite bomb under a bridge at Wattlebridge, on the main Cavan to Clones road about half a mile from the fatal explosion. It was wired and ready for detonation. Donegan and

Gallagher were rushed to Cavan Surgical Hospital. Doctors fought all day to save Donegan's life. Gallagher's injuries, although severe, were not life threatening.

RTÉ carried a report on the main lunchtime news bulletin that a garda inspector had been injured in an explosion on the Cavan border. Sam Donegan's youngest son, Michael, who is now principal of a boys' school in Birr, County Offaly, was then a boarder at St Patrick's College on the edge of Cavan town. He was sitting his Leaving Certificate examination at the time, and heard that his father had been involved in an accident from a day pupil who had returned home for lunch and who heard the news on the radio. Michael's sister, Maura Rosney, was feeding her baby when she also heard the report on the radio. 'They didn't name him but my antennae went up,' she said. 'We rang the guards and they said, yes, it was Daddy, but I never thought he was going to die.'

At home at Highfield Road, Mary was waiting for her husband to call about his dinner. At around 12.30 that afternoon, two gardaí arrived at the door. 'Sam has had an accident,' they told her. 'Put on your coat, he wants to see you.' When they got to Cavan Surgical, the doctors were reluctant to let Mary see him because of the extent of his injuries:

> I told them I had to see him, he was my husband and anyway I had been a nurse. Sam was unconscious. There was a cloth over his arm but when I lifted it, I could see his arm was all blood and his ribs were shattered. And his eye, it was gone. He rallied about three o'clock and told the nurse he was cold. The nurse told me to come quick. He squeezed my hand and said 'Is that yourself?' and he never spoke again. He lapsed back into unconsciousness.

It was around three that afternoon when John Donegan heard that a garda inspector had been injured in an explosion along the border. He was coming to the end of his first year as a teacher in Rathgar in Dublin. He had just returned to his flat and had switched on the radio when he heard the news. Sam Donegan died at five minutes to midnight without regaining consciousness. Maura Rosney recalls driving to the hospital:

> For some reason I didn't think he was that badly hurt. But I remember saying to my husband on the way 'Daddy wouldn't die would he?' He just nodded his head. We got there a moment too late; he had just died. We were devastated. We adored Dad. Mercifully, the hospital had camouflaged his injuries. But I'll always remember the shock of seeing him when he was laid out. They had a plastic bag over his face. I suppose there was a reason for it but the whole thing was unspeakable.

Kathleen Caffrey had been working in the telephone exchange in Dublin that day. When she got word that her father had been hurt in an accident, she rang Cavan and then went straight to the hospital. She was with him when he died. 'I remember the doctors pounding his chest trying to resuscitate him but they couldn't save him.' Frances was on holiday in Wexford when she heard the news. She had been cycling in Kilmore Quay all day, and on her return to her hotel in Rosslare she received an urgent message to call home. On contacting Cavan, her uncle told her that her father had been injured and he would like her to come home. Two Wexford gardaí drove her to Dublin, where a Cavan squad car was waiting to take her home:

They talked about everything and anything on the way up. I wanted to go straight to the hospital but they said 'No, we'll take you home.' When I got there, Maura and her husband were there and we all drove to the hospital. It was around midnight. I ran up the stairs and met my sister, Kathleen, who was on the way down. 'Thank God you're here,' she said. 'Dad has just died.' Next day he was laid out wrapped in white bandages in a mummified manner; we couldn't see his face. He had a white plastic bag over his face, held down with a fine gauze bandage wrapped around and tucked into his habit. I said to the nun 'You can't bury him like that, take that off him' and she said 'Oh I will' but I know they didn't. Ever since, when I dream of him, he has no head; I always have this vision of him sitting at the table or whatever, but I can never see his face.

An inquest would later find that death had been caused by shock consistent with severe blast injuries. Cavan town came to a standstill for Sam Donegan's state funeral. The Garda Band, which some years earlier had been disbanded because of a cost-cutting exercise, had only recently been reformed. Sam Donegan's funeral was the first time that they played after being reformed. There was almost complete silence as the tricolour-draped coffin flanked by twelve uniformed gardaí passed through the streets on the three-mile journey from the cathedral in Cavan to Killygarry Cemetery. At the graveside, a number of young recruits on the guard of honour — some no more than nineteen or twenty — had tears streaming down their faces. 'I don't remember much about that day, things were very blurred, but I can still see them standing there,' recalls Frances McGrath. 'They couldn't wipe away the tears because they were standing to attention. Here they were, just starting out, and it affected them.'

After the burial, Mary Donegan received many letters from elderly people who her husband had visited in the evenings because they were alone. 'We never knew that until he died. He used to check on them to make sure they were alright and after Sam died they wrote to me and told me how much that meant to them and how they would miss him,' she said. 'When Sam died, we were relatively recent arrivals and I have always appreciated how good and caring the people of Cavan have been towards us.' That kindness was the main factor in her decision to keep her home there ever since.

The Irish army were later to confirm that the bomb that killed Sam Donegan was definitely on the Northern side of the border. They were able to tell this from forensic evidence showing that the explosion occurred on the reddish-coloured tarmacadam used to surface roads in the North. The tarmac used for road surfacing in Cavan is black. Because he was killed north of the border, albeit only a few yards into County Fermanagh, the main investigation into the killing of Sam Donegan was handled by the RUC, with some input from the gardaí. Both wings of the IRA, the Provisionals and the Officials, issued statements denying responsibility for planting the bomb. Shortly after the killing, police stopped a car with four men inside, heading in the direction of Belfast. They were questioned about the incident but were allowed to continue their journey. Other people made statements, sources have confirmed, but nothing of any substance materialised.

BETWEEN THE murder of Garda Richard Fallon in 1970 and that of Sam Donegan in 1972, the Northern conflict had exploded and was spilling over into the Republic. The introduction of internment without trial in Northern Ireland in August 1971 had led to widespread confrontation between nationalists and the British security forces, with Belfast and Derry in a state of near-anarchy. In January 1972, British troops had shot dead thirteen civilians and fatally wounded another in Derry on Bloody Sunday. In March, the British government suspended the Northern parliament at Stormont and the first car bomb was detonated in Belfast. The death toll was rising apace. Before the year was out, 496 people were to die in the Northern conflict. Sam Donegan was one of them. The year 1972 had the highest death record in the entire thirty years of the Troubles. It had risen steadily from 18 in 1969, to 28 in 1970, and 180 in 1971. The Official IRA announced a ceasefire in May 1972, but by then the republican split was well and truly complete. By the summer of 1972, there was just one IRA waging an armed campaign — the Provisional IRA. At this stage they were shooting dead, on average, one British soldier every week.

At the start of the campaign the Provisionals depended mainly on explosives. There was no shortage of explosive 'mix', as the IRA had been manufacturing their own. Their methods were crude; a volunteer would simply walk up to the door of an RUC barracks, hang a five- or six-pound bomb on the door, light the fuse and run. They had also begun to blow up border roads to hinder British troops patrolling the area in search of IRA units. The organisation had blown up a number of roads before — and after — the killing of Sam Donegan, but that fact apart, no other evidence has come to light linking the Provisional IRA to the killing.

At the time, loyalist paramilitaries had been making murderous forays into the South. On 1 December 1972, on the night that the Offences Against the State (Amendment) Act was going through the Dáil, loyalists planted a bomb in Dublin city centre, killing two people and injuring 127 others. By 1973, they had killed twelve people in Dublin, Dundalk and elsewhere. Security sources have little doubt, however, that it was the Provos who planted the bomb that killed Sam Donegan. Given that the bomb was placed a few yards into the North, the main target would appear to have been the British army. But this does not explain why they would have detonated it when Donegan and Gallagher came along. Whoever detonated the bomb could have been in no doubt that both were members of the Southern security forces — if they had seen them. Sam Donegan was in full uniform when he was killed, as was John Gallagher, according to a statement issued by the Irish army:

> Lieutenant Gallagher was, at the time, in command of a patrol of soldiers from Cavan military post and was dressed in full uniform. He was carrying a Gustav sub-machine-gun with leather ammunition pouch suspended across his shoulders, both of which are distinctive to the Irish Army and not in use by any other of the forces active in the border area. The military vehicle in which our forces approached the incident bore a tricolour pennant for identification.

In 1972, the IRA were using unsophisticated manual detonators; remote-control devices would come later. There is a strong possibility that whoever detonated the bomb had their vision obscured by the thick bushes and trees bordering Leggikelly

Lane. But this, as with all theories in relation to the killing of Sam Donegan, remains entirely speculative.

SAM DONEGAN had been due to retire in November 1974. He had bought a red Audi nine days before his death. He needed a large car to pull the new caravan he had also just purchased for family holidays, and for himself and Mary when he retired. With the children now grown and most of them self-sufficient, they had been looking forward to having some time to themselves. Gardening was his passion, recalls Mary Donegan:

> Everywhere we went he had wonderful gardens and beehives. He had lots of beehives, he loved them. After he died we found lots of bee-keeping equipment in the attic that he had been gathering for when he retired. But Sam never got to sit in the caravan. He loved going to the Botanic Gardens when he was in Dublin, and second-hand bookshops. He was a great man for books; Greene's bookshop was his favourite. He was very gentle, Sam; he saw good in everyone.

Sam Donegan was born into a farming background in Ballintamper, Ballymacormac, in County Longford in 1911, the second eldest of five boys and two girls. His older brother Joe, a political correspondent and later assistant news editor with the *Irish Press*, was the first journalist in the history of the state to be jailed for refusing to reveal the identity of his sources. This was in 1934, during the de Valera government. He was jailed by the Free State Military Tribunal over refusing to reveal the source of an article that he had written about the Blueshirts. Despite his association with the *Irish Press*, de Valera refused clemency, and the journalist was jailed for a month amid much public furore. He died in 1950 aged forty-one.

The family name was spelled 'Dennigan', but Sam was registered at birth as 'Donegan', an error that came to light only when he joined the gardaí in 1934. He was to meet his future wife when she was a nurse in the fever hospital in County Mayo and he was a patient. He was a young garda stationed at Bellacorick when he became ill with what doctors suspected was diphtheria. As an ambulance nurse, Mary was sent to bring him in to the hospital at Ballina:

> He would not go on the stretcher. The sergeant said to me 'He's a lovely man, but a hellish stubborn one.' He didn't have diphtheria; it was a bad case of tonsillitis. So he was released but he came back to pay his bill and then he asked me to go out with him. He owned a big heavy motorbike and I was always a very nervous passenger.

They married in August 1940 in Mary's home place, Curry, County Sligo. After serving in Partry and Balla in County Mayo, Donegan was promoted to the rank of sergeant in 1952 and was transferred to Achill. By that stage, they had five children. He was transferred to Ballymote, County Sligo, in 1958, to Sligo town in 1965 and, finally, to Cavan on promotion to inspector in December 1967. 'Given his own experience as a young guard, Dad always tried to be kind and helpful to young members starting out,' Frances recalls. 'I have a clear memory of him taking sandwiches and a flask to share with the young guards on border duty.' A couple of weeks before he died, Sam Donegan had bought Frances a new bike for her forthcoming cycling holiday:

He wanted to make sure I had a roadworthy bike so he brought me into Clerys and bought me a Raleigh racer. He tied it onto the front of his car to transport it home to my flat on Waterloo Road. When I was going on holiday he gave me a note to give to the guards in case I needed anything. It said 'This is my daughter, Frances. If she should need anything will you look after her and I will reimburse you?' That's the way he thought of the guards, as if we were one big family. He loved his job. Whenever there were cutbacks, as when the Garda Band went, he'd say: 'There they are, cutting the guards again, it's always the guards.'

Sam Donegan's family meant everything to him, says Frances. They found his death extremely hard to cope with:

Nothing was too good for us; he did everything for us. Then he died and all of a sudden we were alone. When myself, Sheila and Kathleen were living in the flat in Dublin at least one of us would go home every weekend, and he'd often be there to meet us off the bus. He'd make sure we'd have plenty of provisions on our return to Dublin on Sunday and many's the time he'd drive us back to Dublin instead of us having to take the bus.

Financially, life was not easy for Mary Donegan after her husband's death. Their house in Highfield Road was mortgaged and car payments had to be made. Subsequently Mary and her youngest son, Michael, were awarded a total of £8,820 in compensation, £1,520 of which was for Michael's college fees. The rest of the family claimed nothing: they were advised that any award would be deducted from their mother's share. At that time, garda welfare programmes were almost non-existent. The situation has greatly improved over the years, but back then 'the guards were not great at looking after our own,' is how one senior garda put it.

No one told Mary Donegan that she had to continue paying into the garda medical insurance scheme, into which her husband had contributed for thirty-four years. Consequently, her membership lapsed. When health problems arose some years later she made enquiries about joining the medical aid scheme and was told it was not possible to rejoin at that stage. In her mid-sixties, Mrs Donegan was then left without garda medical insurance cover: 'The local gardaí, their families and other members of the force who knew Sam were very helpful and kind at the time. But nobody in an official capacity ever came back and said "How are you doing?" It was just as if he died and that was the end of it.'

Frances McGrath and her sister, Sheila Henry, feel that counselling should have been offered to the family, even belatedly. 'When they discovered the benefits of counselling years later they didn't come back and check with us,' says Frances. 'No one checked the files to see if there was anyone on it like us, who may have benefited from such a service. In all those years, I've never been able to talk about Dad's death; it was too painful. I'd always change the subject. I'm not blaming anyone, it was just the system at that time. We were victims of the time. It's done differently now, thankfully.' Sheila, a teacher and the mother of two sons, feels the loss of her father more deeply as she gets older: 'As I grow older I realise just what I have lost. My sons will never know this man who I adored. As time goes on you appreciate more and more what you had and can never have again. It was an unspeakable tragedy and I feel as if Dad was forgotten, not by us, but by the rest of the world.'

Not knowing who killed Sam Donegan, or why, has not helped his family in coming to terms with what happened on 8 June 1972. 'I remember once going back to Leggikelly Lane,' says Frances. 'There was a big crater in the road. I remember just standing looking at it, this big hole in the road.' It was a radio interview almost thirty years after the death of her father that prompted her to try to find out what exactly happened on the day of the killing:

> All those years I wondered; I always felt there was no closure. I felt that maybe more could have been done to follow it up. One morning, about two years ago, I was listening to the radio and Frank Hand's brother was speaking about the early release of those who had been convicted of his brother's murder. I thought to myself 'In one way you're lucky, you know who killed your brother.' We didn't know who killed Dad. I thought if I saw something on his file, or *something*, I would feel happier. I didn't want to see names — names mean nothing to me — but just the result of their investigation on the day. What time was he sent out, who was with him, what time did the bomb go off? I thought they could show us something.

Sometime later she rang the Garda Commissioner's office and enquired about the investigation file. The Commissioner's office redirected her to the garda archives. They did not have the file either and suggested that she should get back in touch with the Commissioner. Following this, Detective Chief Superintendent Dermot Jennings contacted Frances McGrath, and in January

2001 arranged with a colleague to meet the rest of the family in her house:

> They explained that, because it was never solved, they could show us nothing. People at the time had apparently made statements and, as they were still alive, this precluded them from giving us anything. I asked them could they just tell us what happened that day, or even what organisation they thought was responsible, but they couldn't even tell us that with any certainty. They said they didn't know. I felt they could show us something with the names blocked out, but no. When they were leaving they said they'd get back to us in a couple of weeks. I said 'There's no hurry, we've waited thirty years, we can wait another while.' They were extremely kind and earned the appreciation of the family, but to date nothing has come of that meeting.

In 1997, during the celebration of the seventy-fifth anniversary of the establishment of the Garda Síochána, the Garda Commissioner invited the Donegan family to garda headquarters for a Mass in honour of all the gardaí who had been killed in the line of duty. They were also invited to the Garda Training College at Templemore for a courtesy visit. Mary and some family members went down to Templemore and saw Sam Donegan's name inscribed on the roll of honour. But while these tributes are welcome, they do little to dim the sense of loss experienced by the Donegan family, which is still evident three decades later:

Do you know, I can still see Sam that day, standing at the glass case drinking his cup of tea and looking for his wellingtons? After he was killed they brought me back those wellingtons; they were in with other things belonging to him. He was a very gentle man, Sam; he didn't deserve what happened to him. Louise was the only grandchild he ever saw; there are twenty now and one great-grandchild. He would have loved them. Sam missed all of that.

The garda authorities remain tight-lipped about what happened at Leggikelly Lane on 8 June 1972. They say the file has not been closed. The investigation, they say, is 'ongoing'.

3

Garda Michael Reynolds

~~~~~~~~

ublin in the early 1970s was a good place to be for the
radically inclined. It was a period of huge socio-
economic and political change, and of significant social
upheaval. Demonstrations against high taxation, low wages,
poor housing, the contraception ban and nearly everything in
between were taking place almost on a weekly basis. Housing
action groups had sprung up and were busily taking over
buildings in organised sit-ins from which they had to be forcibly
removed. On top of this, the Northern conflict had broken out
and was spilling over into the South in the form of bank
robberies and other incidents.

In the middle of this maelstrom was a young couple named
Noel and Marie Murray. They had met at an Official Sinn Féin
meeting and married in 1973. They later fell out with the
Officials when that organisation moved totally away from
republicanism and adopted a purely Marxist position. The
Murrays were not republicans in the traditional sense: anarchists
would be a more accurate description. They were attached to a

loose alliance of left-wingers who used to staff citizens' advice centres in Dublin's inner city and outlying suburbs. Around 1973 and 74, the Murrays were very active in the Crumlin area of south Dublin in what sources close to the couple describe as the 'back end of the housing protests'. Crumlin was a few miles from Ranelagh's flatland where the couple had lived in rented accommodation.

Marie Murray was a civil servant from Castlepollard in County Westmeath. She was an intelligent woman who had achieved straight honours in her Leaving Certificate. After school, she walked into a job in the Department of the Gaeltacht. She was working there when she met Noel Murray but left on the eve of her marriage. He was from Celbridge in County Kildare and from a working-class background. In the late 1960s, he worked as a metal fabricator with Córas Iompair Éireann. He left CIÉ and began working in the private sector with a firm of fabricators in Tallaght, County Dublin. In 1974, Noel Murray was on the run: a number of warrants had been issued for his arrest for possession of explosives and firearms and for robbery. His wife was slightly built, about five feet four inches tall with small, fine features and glasses. He was tall and thin with longish hair and a quiet manner. They were just eight months into their marriage when Marie Murray was charged with receiving £500, the proceeds of a payroll robbery from Contract Cleaners in Dublin. In July 1974, the Special Criminal Court sentenced her to twenty-four months in jail, suspended on condition that she keep the peace for two years. This was Marie Murray's first serious brush with the gardaí.

MICHAEL REYNOLDS was a young uniformed garda from Ballinasloe in County Galway. He had joined the gardaí in 1970 at the age of twenty-four, and in 1975 was stationed at Clontarf Garda Station on the north side of Dublin. His patch extended almost as far as Howth, towards the very north of the capital. He was married and had a baby daughter aged two. He was known as a tough law and order man and a stickler for handing out tickets for road traffic and other minor violations. On many an occasion he issued tickets for parking or car tax to people he knew well, shopkeepers and others he met almost on a daily basis. To Michael Reynolds, the law was the law and was not to be flouted by anyone, in any measure. In Reynolds' book, there was no such thing as a minor offence.

In September 1975, Garda Reynolds was rostered for night duty in Clontarf. The shifts started at 10 p.m. and ended at 6 a.m. the following day. On Thursday, 11 September, he finished his shift, drove the two miles home to Ardmore Drive in Artane and went to bed. He got up earlier than usual, as he wanted to go to the garda station to pick up his pay cheque and then go to the bank to have it cashed. When he got up he had a late, leisurely breakfast and promised to go shopping with his wife, Vera.

At Ballsbridge, on the other side of the city, two men were in the car park in front of the Hospitals Sweepstakes building. It was 1.45 p.m. They were sizing up a 1970 green Ford Cortina. It was a company car. Its owner, Ross Connolly, used to park there regularly while he was at work. One of the men tampered with the door lock and it opened easily. He slid into the driver's seat and opened the door at the passenger side to let his companion in. They started the car without any problem and drove quickly through the gates and out onto the Merrion Road. They headed in the direction of Killester, just beyond Clontarf. At around four that afternoon, the Cortina pulled to a halt outside the Killester branch of the Bank of Ireland, on Howth Road, with its four wheels on the footpath. The driver remained behind the wheel with the engine running while three passengers jumped out and ran into the bank, leaving two of the car doors hanging open.

Inside the bank the three spread out and pulled out guns: 'This is a raid,' shouted one of the raiders as shocked staff looked up in alarm. Levelling his gun at the staff he ordered them to move back from the counter. 'Don't panic and no one will get hurt.' He had a green woollen mask with slits across the eyes. There was one woman, slightly built and with long blonde hair which witnesses would later say resembled a wig. Carrying a revolver in her left hand, she vaulted the counter, pushing past a female teller, Deirdre Stevenson. The raider was holding a brown bag in her right hand, into which she began stuffing wads of cash as quickly as she could, while all the time keeping the gun trained on Stevenson.

John Dawson, the bank manager, was in his office finishing an interview with the only customer left in the bank at the time. His door was kicked in. 'Put up your hands and don't attempt to set off the alarm,' one of the raiders ordered. 'If you do this, nobody will get hurt.' On the floor of the bank, a teller, Patricia Horan, felt faint with the shock. A colleague brought her to a desk and laid her head on it. A male raider noticed: 'Don't cry,' he said, 'no one will get hurt.' The three raiders then made for the door with the bags of cash. 'No alarms and thanks,' said one, running out the door to the waiting Cortina.

The Killester branch was wired to both Raheny Garda Station and Chubb Alarms' headquarters. The alarm had somehow been tripped and it was now going off in Chubb's

South Leinster Street offices. The gardaí were also receiving warnings about a bank raid in progress. The first call was logged at 4.02 p.m., just as the raiders were escaping with £7,059 in Irish and English notes. The biggest chunk of cash, £1,605, was in Irish £5 notes. There was also £750 in English £5 notes and £380 in Irish £20 notes. The raiders had also scooped up miscellaneous currency, including notes from the Bank of Scotland and Ulster Bank. The haul included one very rare Hibernian £1 note.

Shortly after three that afternoon, Michael Reynolds left his house with his wife and child and climbed into the family's yellow Vauxhall Viva. Vera Reynolds put baby Emer on her lap and put a cassette in the tape deck. At around four o'clock the Reynoldses were coming up to Killester Shopping Centre when a green car lurched onto the road in front of their car, forcing Michael Reynolds to swerve to avoid it. He blasted his horn but the car was already speeding off in the opposite direction. 'I bet that's a stolen car,' said the garda, turning his head towards his wife while at the same time turning the car in the same direction as the green Cortina. 'Be careful,' Vera Reynolds urged, 'they might have guns.' Her husband just laughed and told her there was nothing to worry about. Sure hadn't he been a patrol driver?

By this stage, gardaí were responding to the alarm calls and were speeding towards the bank with sirens blazing. A deliveryman, who had been passing the bank, saw the raiders running out, realised what had just happened and had the foresight to jot down the car registration number. Michael Reynolds, who was now catching up on the gang's Cortina, began blowing his horn. There was panic inside the raiders' car. 'Faster, go faster,' they were shouting as the driver accelerated through the busy streets at about sixty miles per hour. The Cortina swerved onto Dunseverick Road, onto Castle Grove, turning left again at Castle Avenue, right onto Vernon Avenue and left at Sybil Hill Road. It then turned sharply into St Anne's Park in Raheny. Reynolds' car was close behind.

A young girl, Lucia McMahon, was playing in the park near the clock tower when she saw a car speeding towards her. It took the corner on two wheels, screeched to a halt under a clump of trees and ended up on the grass to the left of the clock tower. Four people got out; three ran along the pathway and one made for the open green. Michael Reynolds had been ready to jump from his own car before the Cortina stopped. He chased the raider who was running across the grass. Lucia McMahon saw the raiders running along near the bank of a small river. One of them was pulling along another who showed signs of tiring. Then a woman's voice shouted, 'Let go my fellow.' McMahon then heard a loud bang like planks of wood falling.

An eleven-year-old boy, Rory McKinley, had also been in the park playing with a friend near the bridge when he heard the bang. He saw three men, one with a long, drooping moustache, and one woman. Moments before the children heard the bang, Reynolds had dived on a male raider and the two fell struggling onto the grassy knoll beside the river. One of the raiders opened fire with a Colt .45 and pumped a bullet into Reynolds' head. Spinning, he hit the ground face up, bleeding profusely from a wound to the head. The garda lay unconscious near the small river with his feet in the water. There was a hole in his forehead, and his eyes were closed. Blood pouring from his mouth and nose was streaming down his face and onto his T-shirt.

Squad cars were now arriving in St Anne's Park. For twenty agonising minutes, Vera Reynolds waited by the car with her baby in her arms while gardaí saturated the area. A plain-clothes officer came along and she asked him if Mick was okay. He did not know her husband, he replied, but he had seen a man lying in a pool of blood in the ditch. 'I knew it was Mick,' she said. In an interview with the *Irish Press* shortly after her husband's murder, Vera Reynolds described how she had waited in the car with her daughter when Garda Reynolds ran after the bank robbers:

> My husband went after them and I waited in the car with Emer. I was waiting only a few minutes when I thought I heard a shot, but I wasn't sure. I thought it might have come from the cassette, which was playing in the car. I didn't want to leave the baby but when Mick didn't return I got out of the car and walked into the park. There were two young lads standing under a tree and I asked them if they had heard a shot, but they said that they hadn't. The two of them then went to see what had happened.

Michael Reynolds was taken by ambulance to the casualty department of Jervis Street Hospital and rushed into theatre, but there was nothing that the doctors could do to save him. He died at 6.10 that evening. A post-mortem revealed that the entry wound had penetrated the frontal bone of the skull slightly to the left of the forehead. Death was caused by laceration of the brain consistent with fractures of the skull from the gunshot wound. Vera Reynolds was at home in Ardmore Drive minding the baby when she heard the news of her husband's death on the radio. She had not gone in the ambulance with him because the gardaí had assured her that he would be okay.

Reynolds' colleagues in Clontarf Garda Station were stunned when they heard that he had been shot dead. Sergeant Dan McHale, who had worked with Reynolds for a couple of years, was particularly upset: 'He was utterly conscientious in his work but terribly generous to people in trouble. His death is a great personal loss to us all,' he said of his slain colleague.

SHORTLY AFTER the murder, gardaí threw a drag-net around the park and immediate area. All available detectives were drafted in for the murder investigation, backed up by troops, tracker dogs, ballistics experts and an Air Corps helicopter. By early evening on the day of the shooting, more than one hundred officers and troops were combing St Anne's Park for clues. John Joy, the head of the Garda Special Branch, and Patrick Culligan, who later went on to become Garda Commissioner, led the investigation. They set up an incident room at Raheny Garda Station, but the hunt also involved checking suspects on files of known subversives at garda headquarters. The bullet had been removed from Garda Reynolds and sent for forensic examination. The getaway car had also been removed by tow wagon to the technical bureau at headquarters.

By this stage, gardaí had traced the getaway car and were interviewing its owner, Ross Connolly. When he eventually got to look at it, after it had been forensically examined for fingerprints and other evidence, he identified a number of items that did not belong to him or his family. According to a garda report, they included a woman's dark blue handbag; a blue and white imitation leather holder for contact lens; a nylon hairbrush; a false moustache; part of a woman's nylon stocking; a blue coat button; a biro and a bunch of keys. An inch-by-inch search of St Anne's Park yielded many items including two knives — not thought to be linked to the crime — and two gloves.

All four raiders had managed to escape before the gardaí sealed off St Anne's Park. Nobody noticed the lone woman crossing the road to the 29A bus stop. It was the female raider, Marie Murray. She stood nervously at the bus stop as a squad car drove by. Its occupants did not give her a second glance. By the time she returned home, the second raider was there. He was her husband, Noel Murray. They both listened to the news bulletin on the radio. It led with the breaking news that Garda Michael Reynolds had died from his injuries.

The government put up a reward of £20,000 for information leading to the arrest of Garda Reynolds' killers, and the gardaí issued detailed descriptions of four people whom they wanted to question, followed by photofit pictures of three of the gang members. Within a day of the shooting, gardaí had logged hundreds of calls, many of which proved to be useless. The Provisional IRA had also issued a statement denying responsibility for the murder. On the evening of 12 September, Michael Reynolds' body was taken to Mount Argus church where hundreds of mourners were waiting. Vera Reynolds carried a small pink posy from her daughter with the simple message: 'To Daddy from Emer'.

The following morning, the dead garda was taken back to Ballinasloe to be buried in his home place. The acting garda chaplain, Fr Clarence Daly, told the mourners that Garda Michael Reynolds had died a courageous man: 'It was this dedication to duty that dictated his actions that Thursday afternoon. He was a dedicated man, a brave man, a fearless man.'

ON 14 September, the day after Garda Reynolds' funeral, Christina Doyle was at work cleaning the public toilets on

Marine Road, in Dún Laoghaire. She had just gone into one of the cubicles when something caught her eye. It was a large brown-paper laundry bag from the Terenure Laundry on the south side of Dublin. Something made her decide to put it into her locker to look at later. She clocked off at 10 p.m. and opened the bag. Inside it were two brown-coloured pillowcases, a false moustache, a man's gabardine jacket, a grey balaclava and some paper cash-bags from the Bank of Ireland. One of the pillowcases opened slightly and a single pound note wafted silently to the ground. The Marine Road toilets were located close to the Sealink ferry terminal and the railway line. The massive publicity surrounding the Reynolds killing was still fresh in Christina Doyle's mind, so she rang the gardaí. Doyle did not know it, but the laundry bag was the first break in the case.

Gardaí began to examine their lists of suspects to see if anyone fitting the raiders' description lived in the vicinity of Dún Laoghaire, although it was also possible that whoever had killed Michael Reynolds had fled the country, aware that the penalty for capital murder was death. On 23 September, gardaí arrested twenty-five-year-old Ronald Damian Stenson, of St Aiden's Park Road, Marino. Stenson was a friend of the Murrays. During questioning at Clontarf Garda Station, Stenson said he had not seen Noel Murray since he had gone on the run on the explosives charges. He had been at home all afternoon on the day of the killing and only heard about it on the radio, he said. The gardaí let him go — for now.

That week, detectives got their second, and most crucial, lead in the case. The offer of a reward was starting to pay off. One of the calls that had come in was from a man who had known Marie Murray. He had identified her from a picture that a detective had shown to him. The only problem was the name: he knew her as Ann Finlay.

Finding an address for Marie Murray was also proving problematic. The couple had moved from Ranelagh and were now living at Grangemore Estate in Raheny. Eventually, the gardaí tracked her down. In a dawn raid on 8 October, detectives from the Special Branch forced open the door to the Murrays' rented semi-detached home, located in a quiet cul-de-sac. Gardaí were upstairs searching for anything linking the Murrays to the Reynolds killing when Detective Garda Brian Kelly looked out the bedroom window. It was 8 a.m. The Murrays were walking up the road with an Alsatian dog on a lead. Noel Murray opened the door and as the couple went into the hallway they found themselves looking down the barrel of a sub-machine-gun. When Detective Inspector Myles Hawkshaw searched Noel Murray he found a gun and a matchbox containing a number of bullets in his jacket pocket. He asked the suspect if there were any other guns hidden in the house. Murray took him upstairs to the back bedroom and there, hidden under a mattress, was a Colt .45 revolver. He then directed Hawkshaw towards a hot press where detonators had been stored.

Detectives then turned the house upside down. They ransacked it until late that afternoon. They found six fuses, two copper pipe bombs and six sticks of Frangex — a transportable type of gelignite — in the bottom drawer of the fridge. They also found a large blue suitcase containing two bags, one paper and one plastic. The bags were stuffed with cash, thousands of pounds in Irish and English currency. On the same day, gardaí returned to Stenson's house with a warrant. They searched the house and, after a struggle, Stenson was taken into custody.

As the Murrays were driven away for questioning to separate garda stations, fingerprint experts were called in to examine the banknotes found in the suitcase. The same experts had found no fingerprints in the bank at Killester. Four pieces of paper used to bind the notes matched Noel Murray's prints, which had been taken while he was in garda custody. Marie Murray's right thumbprint on another piece of paper also matched her palm mark taken from the paper bag containing the cash. The forensic evidence against the couple was building up. The next step was to bring the cash found in the Murrays' house to the bank in Killester. When two bank officials counted the money it added up to a little more than £7,000, almost the exact amount that had been stolen on 11 September.

Other, apparently innocent, items were proving valuable in putting the Murrays at the scene of the bank raid. The hairbrush that had been found in the stolen car was traced to a shop in Donaghmede, near to where the Murrays lived. The large blue button retrieved from the getaway car matched the buttons on a blue coat found in the attic of the Murrays' home: the top button of the coat was missing. The left-hand black glove found in the park matched a right-hand glove found in Grangemore Estate. Most important of all, the bullet taken from Garda Reynolds' body matched a .45 casing found at the scene *and* the gun retrieved from the Murrays' bedroom. The state forensic scientist, Dr James Donovan, concluded that the casing and the bullet had come from the same batch. There was now an established link between five crucial sites: the Killester bank, St Anne's Park, the green Cortina, the toilet in Dún Laoghaire and Grangemore Estate.

Tests on the Colt .45 showed that the revolver had two safety catches, one on the left side of the gun and the other on the butt of the handle. Both were working perfectly. The tests revealed that it would be impossible for the gun to go off accidentally, as the person pressing the trigger would have to apply seven pounds of pressure to make it fire. Noel Murray was being held at Harcourt Terrace Garda Station. Detectives asked him if he owned the gun. No, he said, he was just minding it for someone else. 'We believe you can help with our enquiries into the Killester bank robbery,' said one detective. 'I can't help you, I can't help you,' Murray responded. Detective Inspector Edward Ryan then came into the interview room and asked Murray if he knew Ronald Stenson. 'Yes,' he replied. Ryan left the room briefly and then returned: 'Why did you not tell me about the gelignite in the fridge?' he asked.

Marie Murray, meanwhile, was in Ballymun Garda Station, some ten miles away. She refused to answer questions at first. When asked specifically who fired the fatal shot, she said 'Circumstances make it impossible to tell you that.' Detectives then decided to take her back to St Anne's Park: returning to the scene of the crime might help refresh her memory. They drove her to the park in an unmarked garda car. Murray looked out the window for most of the journey. When they arrived at St Anne's she refused point-blank to go in. 'I'm not going to walk into that park,' she said. They took her back to the garda station and gave her some tea.

Shortly after 1 p.m., Detective Inspector John Finlay came into Marie Murray's holding cell. He asked her if she was now prepared to make a statement. Yes, she said. Finlay spent four hours writing down the statement, but when it was complete, Murray refused to sign it. Detectives then asked her to identify a number of items, including the false moustaches and balaclavas worn by the male bank raiders, the handbag found in the Cortina, the suitcase used to store the stolen cash and the blue button from the coat which, it would transpire, she had worn on the day of the raid. In the unsigned statement — which she later contested in court — Murray said that a few days before the bank robbery she and her husband had met two men and the four of them planned the bank job. The men were to provide the getaway car, while she and Noel would provide the guns. The Murrays and another raider went into the bank, while the fourth man remained at the wheel. They drove into St Anne's Park and abandoned the car. She was running, carrying two guns and trying to keep pace with the other raiders, when she saw a 'very fit looking man' tackling Noel to the ground:

> I was panicking and I screamed, 'Let go my fellow.' All I could think of was that Noel was caught and I moved in to take Noel away from him … I am not clear what happened. I think I made a swipe at the man with my right hand. This was the hand in which I had the big gun. It was a Colt .45. [This had been given to her by Noel, fully loaded with a bullet in the breech and the safety catch off.] Obviously I had not put the safety catch on. As I made the swipe my gun went off, there was a shot and the man crumpled up. I could not believe what happened. The man was there one minute and next he was down. After this I don't know. I never intended to hurt anyone. It did not register with me that he had actually been shot. You cannot believe you have done anything like that. Everyone scattered and I ran alone, feeling unreal.

At around six that evening, Marie Murray was driven across the city under armed guard to Harcourt Terrace, where Noel Murray was being held. The two were brought into the same room where they spoke for about thirty minutes, alone, although gardaí were outside the window in the laneway. Marie Murray would later deny that she had made a statement. Either way, there were more than a few holes in her story. The post-mortem had shown no evidence of burning or powder marks around the wound on Michael Reynolds' head, as it would have done had he been shot at close range as Murray suggested when she claimed to have made a swipe at him. Also, as mentioned, tests on the gun revealed that the killer would have needed to apply at least seven pounds of pressure to activate the trigger, thus ruling out the possibility that it had been fired accidentally.

Three hours after Marie Murray had been removed from the room, Noel Murray had a visit from his counsel, Brian Doolan. They made out a statement saying that Murray did not wish to make oral or written statements in connection with the murder of Michael Reynolds or other offences. It was signed N.A. Murray. Noel Murray made another statement (which he later contested) detailing the discovery of items found in his house at the time of his arrest on 8 October. Detectives meanwhile had sent a file to the Director of Public Prosecutions. Noel and Marie Murray and Ronald Stenson were charged with capital murder and armed robbery. The Murrays were also charged with possession of firearms and explosives. Of the fourth raider — 'Johnny' — there was no sign.

THE TRIAL opened in the Special Criminal Court in May 1976 amid a blaze of publicity. Noel and Marie Murray were the first — and only — husband and wife in the history of the state to stand trial for capital murder. In those days, for a female to have a whiff of cordite around her was extraordinary and there was much speculation about whether or not the state would actually execute a woman. The general feeling was that anyone convicted of the murder of Garda Reynolds would hang. From the outset of the trial, Noel and Marie Murray claimed that two statements which the court had accepted in evidence had been made under duress, physical in his case and verbal in hers. Noel Murray claimed that the money found in his house in the October raid was the proceeds of a collection, and not a bank robbery: 'The prosecution case is that the money found in my home was from a bank raid. This money was from collections made for the anarchist movement, Black X. I intend to claim it. I want it back. This money was intended for prisoners' relief.'

Bangharda Sarah McGuinness was among the first garda witnesses for the prosecution. She was one of the female officers who had dealings with Marie Murray while she was in custody. During that time, the prisoner had admitted killing Garda Reynolds, McGuinness said. 'She [Murray] mentioned the bank raid and said "You know what happened after that. I did it. You know that." I asked her if she knew he was a guard. She said she did not, that she heard it on the news. She said he caught one of them. She only intended to hit him. He crumpled up. It was all terrible. She said there was panic and confusion.'

When it was her turn in the witness box, Marie Murray admitted making a statement, which she now described as untrue: 'I suppose I laid it on a bit thick. But I felt I had to dramatise it to protect Noel. They [the gardaí] wanted me to name a fourth person and suggested that I was protecting this person because I was carrying on with him. To put it in a nutshell, they called me a whore.'

The Murray trial turned into one of the stormiest in Irish legal history. Heated arguments broke out on a number of occasions, defence counsel withdrew from the case midway through and the co-accused, Ronald Stenson, collapsed semiconscious in the dock. A psychiatrist was called in. (Subsequently, Stenson was tried separately and acquitted of all charges.) As Brian Doolan and the other defence counsel left the courtroom, the Murrays began roaring and demanded a new trial before a new court — or tribunal, as they insisted on calling it. Noel Murray told the court that he and his wife were anarchists whose 'only purpose in this state is to destroy it'.

'This trial is a charade and a farce. I want a separate trial,' his wife shouted at the bench. 'Fascist pigs,' she roared, 'all you are are state prosecutors and you've broken Stenson.' She was still shouting as warders and Special Branch detectives pounced on her and forced her struggling to the cells below. At that moment, Noel Murray jammed his feet against the dock and had to be forcibly removed. From that point on, the Murrays listened to the proceedings through specially installed speakers in the holding cell underneath the dock.

The evidence against the Murrays, circumstantial and forensic, proved overwhelming. On 9 June, the three judges found the self-confessed anarchists, Noel and Marie Murray, guilty on all counts. (The other two raiders were never found.) In an hour-long résumé of the trial, Mr Justice Denis Pringle, presiding, ruled out 'any factual basis' for the Murrays' claim that their statements had been obtained under duress. On the killing of Garda Reynolds, he said that a person was guilty of capital murder if the perpetrator had known or ought to have known at the time of the killing that the victim was a garda. The court imposed sentences of thirty-five years on the charges of bank robbery and possession of firearms and explosives. On the capital murder of Garda Michael Reynolds there was only one sentence open to the court once it had found the accused guilty — death by hanging.

Marie Murray was first up from the cell to hear the sentence passed.

'Have you anything to say?' the judge asked.

'No sentence you can give is justified because this is not a court,' she retorted. As she was led back down the steps she shouted, 'Are you afraid of what we may have to say?' The double execution was scheduled for 9 July.

THE MURRAYS were taken away, Noel to the Curragh Prison in County Kildare and his wife to Mountjoy Jail in Dublin. They were to spend six months in the condemned cell. Marie Murray was on round-the-clock lock-up, guarded by three female jailers. Each night, for six months, the warders were locked in with her. A chemical toilet had been installed for the warders' benefit. A major talking-point during this period was the availability of an official hangman, in the event that the government would refuse to commute the death sentence to one of forty years' imprisonment. The fact that Liam Cosgrave's strongly conservative Fine Gael was in power (in coalition with the Labour Party) added to the belief that the executions would go ahead. Sources close to the Murrays indicated that the couple themselves believed they were going to be executed. And public statements uttered by gardaí — and the RUC — made it clear that a significant number of police officers on both sides of the border would shed no tears if they were to die by the hangman's rope.

The mood on the streets was entirely different. Almost as soon as the verdict had been announced, friends of the couple began a campaign demanding the lifting of the death sentence. Dr Miriam Daly of Queen's University Belfast opened a defence fund to cover the couple's legal bill, and for almost six months civil liberties groups organised well-attended protest marches in the capital. Even twenty-five years ago, it appears, the majority of Irish people were totally against the death penalty. The Special Criminal Court subsequently granted a stay of execution, which, in the light of what was to happen, was just as well.

In December 1976 Noel and Marie Murray appealed the convictions to the Supreme Court on the basis that they had not known that Michael Reynolds was a garda, and they therefore could not be guilty of capital murder. In a landmark ruling, five judges of the Supreme Court upheld the appeal — the Special Criminal Court had got it wrong. They had no difficulty quashing the capital murder conviction and death sentence on Noel Murray, replacing it with a conviction of common law murder. In the case of his wife, they ordered a retrial, as it was she who had pulled the trigger. There was no doubt that both were guilty of murder. The key point was: did the prosecution have the required proof of knowledge to sustain a capital murder conviction?

'It would be repugnant to reason and fairness if the death penalty were to depend on the outcome of what, in effect, would have been a lottery as to the victim's occupation and activity,' said Mr Justice Seamus Henchy, delivering the judgment. Marie Murray's retrial, he said, must be approached on the basis that there was no evidence that she knew the victim was a garda. If she did not know — and there had been nothing to indicate that Michael Reynolds was a garda, as he was in civilian clothes — then she could not be guilty of capital murder. At the retrial in April 1977, the capital murder charge was overturned, but she was found guilty of murder and sentenced to life imprisonment. The Murray case made legal history, as it clarified the standard of proof necessary to sustain a capital murder conviction.

In the final outcome, nothing turned on who had actually pulled the trigger, as in law both were equally guilty. Marie Murray had admitted in court that she had tailored her statement to protect her husband. It is entirely possible that it was he who fired the shot, not his wife. Witnesses had given sworn evidence of seeing her tiring and having to be helped along. Marie Murray was carrying the bag of cash. It is unlikely that, as the weakest of the four, she would also have been lumbered with two heavy firearms. Could it be that she had taken the rap in the belief that a woman would be less likely to be hanged than a man? The only two people who know the truth are the Murrays themselves, but they are not saying.

During their time in prison, the couple brought a High Court action seeking permission for closed prison visits to allow them to have children. The action failed. Marie Murray obtained a degree in English from London University and made it to the finals of a short story competition. She went on to do a Higher Diploma in Education at Trinity College Dublin after the prison authorities permitted her to attend outside lectures. She would leave a bicycle at a friend's house on the North Circular Road, collect it and cycle down to College Green for lectures. Towards the end of his sentence, Noel Murray spent time in the training unit at Mountjoy. He also was granted short periods of temporary release.

The couple were released on licence, or conditional release, in July 1992. They had spent almost seventeen years behind bars. Since then, Marie Murray has worked in a variety of courier jobs. Her husband has also returned to the workforce. When this author contacted the Murrays they declined to be interviewed, as they felt it may contravene their licence and possibly jeopardise their chance of securing a full, unconditional release. They now live in a neat, end-of-terrace house in a Leinster housing estate, with their two pet dogs. They never had any children. Noel and Marie Murray are known to regret what happened that day in St Anne's Park twenty-six years ago. They are, according to sources close to the couple, 'just getting on with life'.

4

Garda Michael Clerkin

Click Clerkin
I remember our days together
And resurrect them from their
Comfortable sleeping place in the clay
Evelyn Conlon[1]

Nineteen seventy-five and early 1976 was a period of disillusionment for the Provisional IRA. A brief, and — from the Provos' point of view — fruitless, IRA ceasefire had ended in bloodshed. It was a period when the IRA was fragmented and came closest to defeat. On 1 March 1976, the British Labour government abolished political status for paramilitary prisoners, and several republicans in Long Kesh began a blanket protest that was to end in hunger strike. The conflict in the prisons proved to be a life-saving kiss for the Provisionals. As 1976 wore on, the situation in the North

1 From Evelyn Conlon, *Thoughts Among the Bindies* (1973).

seemed to be spiralling out of control as both sides indulged in an orgy of sectarian killings. That year the British SAS was used for the first time in Northern Ireland. With 308 deaths, 1976 had the second highest number of fatalities of the Troubles. In seven months, between 1 January and 21 July 1976, 200 people were killed in the conflict. In the Republic, Noel and Marie Murray were under threat of execution for the murder of Garda Michael Reynolds, and the strongly conservative Fine Gael-led Cosgrave coalition government was in power.

On 21 July, the IRA assassinated the British Ambassador to Ireland, Christopher Ewart-Biggs, in Dublin. He had been in office just twelve days when his car was blown up by a landmine as he left his official residence in Sandyford, County Dublin, shortly before 10 a.m. His Jaguar car, which had been fitted with armour plating, was thrown into the air by the blast. Judith Cooke, a British civil servant working at the Northern Ireland Office, was also killed in the explosion caused by the 200-pound device. In the aftermath of the assassination, the Irish government declared a state of emergency and announced the introduction of additional security measures aimed at the IRA. One of these was the Criminal Law Act, which increased the penalty for IRA membership from two to seven years and provided for a range of new offences, including recruiting.

A second, more controversial — and oppressive — piece of legislation was the Emergency Powers Bill. This, the government envisaged, would supplement the Offences Against the State Act and the Criminal Law Act and effectively put the IRA out of business in the South. One of the measures contained in the new bill allowed the gardaí to hold suspects for up to seven days without charge. The Provos were naturally opposed to its introduction, but it also provoked strong opposition among the general public. The President of Ireland, Cearbhall Ó Dálaigh, who was a very distinguished former Chief Justice, refused to sign the bill into law without first referring it to the Supreme Court to test its constitutionality. The Supreme Court ruled it constitutional and sent it back to the President for his signature. Shortly after midnight on Saturday, 16 October, Ó Dálaigh signed the new bill into law. Fifty minutes later, the Provos gave their response to the Emergency Powers Act. They killed an unarmed garda, Michael Clerkin, in a booby-trap explosion at Garryhinch, near Mountmellick in County Laois. He was just twenty-four years old.

MICHAEL CLERKIN was a single man from Monaghan town and had been a garda for just four years when he was killed. He was a good-looking man, about five feet ten inches tall, with thick dark hair and a moustache. His first station was Portarlington in County Laois, but in January 1975 he was seconded from there to Portlaoise Prison for fifteen months, to the communications room. He returned to Portarlington in April 1976, but had heard that he was to be detailed to the prison full-time. The young garda hated prison duty, mainly because Portlaoise housed paramilitary prisoners. For someone as apolitical as Michael Clerkin was, the prison posting was an anathema. All he wanted was to be an ordinary garda on the beat. He applied for a transfer, and in October 1976 was waiting on word to come through. In Áras an Uachtaráin in Dublin, President Ó Dálaigh was preparing to sign the Emergency Powers Bill into law. It was twenty minutes to midnight on Friday, 15 October. At that moment a call came through to Portlaoise Garda Station. An anonymous woman was on the line with a cryptic message. The call, the gardaí believed, came from Portarlington. She told the garda on duty that she had seen a number of men acting suspiciously around a disused house at Garryhinch: would the gardaí come and check it out? She also mumbled something about an assassination plot against Oliver J. Flanagan, the Fine Gael TD who lived in nearby Mountmellick.

Michael Clerkin was on duty at Portarlington Garda Station that Friday night. Garda Paddy Egan had offered to swap shifts with Clerkin to let the young garda go out for the night with his girlfriend, Betty Cooper. Clerkin thanked Egan for the offer, but said he would do the shift as normal. Portlaoise radioed through to the sergeant-in-charge in Portarlington, Jim Cannon, telling him about the call that had just been received. Cannon, Clerkin and Garda Gerry Bohan waited at The Square in Portarlington for two armed officers to arrive from Portlaoise, detective gardaí Ben Thornton and Thomas Peters. Thornton and Peters travelled the three miles to Garryhinch in an unmarked car. Clerkin drove the patrol car with the other two uniformed officers inside. The isolated stone and mortar two-storey house was located about two hundred yards up a laneway off a side road near the main Portarlington to Mountmellick road. It belonged to a local farmer who had not lived there for about a year and it was lying idle.

Peters pulled up in front of the house and Clerkin parked on the road. The five gardaí checked the outside of the house as best they could, using high-powered torches. They saw nothing suspicious and then moved in to check the interior of the house. Cannon, Clerkin, Bohan and Thornton went to the back of the house, while Peters remained at the front. Thornton then went around to the front again. Cannon and Bohan were still at the back of the house, at the gable end, when Thornton and Peters went in through the front door. Seconds later, Clerkin got in through a ground-floor window at the back. The young garda turned slightly to his left and stepped onto a flagstone when, suddenly, there was an enormous explosion. Clerkin had stepped directly onto a bomb that had been planted underneath a flagstone slightly to the left of the rear door.

The huge blast ripped through the house, collapsing the entire building. Debris and mortar flew everywhere. It rained down on the men inside and outside the house and on the squad cars, almost crushing one of them. Sergeant Cannon, who was buried up to his neck in mortar, watched in horror as huge lumps of rock and masonry rained down upon his colleagues. He and Bohan had been trapped close to each other in the rubble, but their hands were free so they were able to lift the masonry off their bodies. When the sergeant tried to stand he realised that his legs had been injured, but the soft mortar and plaster had formed a cushion, so he escaped without a single broken bone. His garda cap was blown into bushes several hundred feet away.

Jim Cannon heard moaning and groans of pain coming from underneath the wreckage of the middle of the house. He stumbled around in the dark and saw the bloodied face of Thomas Peters lying partially covered by rocks and other debris. He was clearing the rocks from Peters' upper body and from around his mouth to allow him to breathe when he heard the sound of moans coming from the centre of the house, where the pile of rubble was about eight feet deep. Cannon knew that one of his colleagues was buried underneath and he tried to remove some of the rocks but the rubble was too deep. He went to the garda radio to call for help but the blast had blown off the ariel.

Garda Bohan, meanwhile, was making his way to a farm about two hundred yards away from the scene of the explosion.

The farmer, Billy Moore, had been in bed when he heard what sounded like two explosions and was wondering what the noise was when Bohan pounded on the door. The blast had been heard as far away as Portlaoise, six miles from the scene of the explosion. One garda who heard it thought it was the prison, as the alarm had been raised. When Billy Moore opened the door he saw Gerry Bohan standing there with blood streaming down his face. His clothes were saturated with blood and bits of dust and mortar. Three of his colleagues were dying, he told Moore; they were trapped under the debris. Moore called two of his brothers and the three ran towards the wrecked house.

When the first squad car arrived at the scene, its occupants found Gerry Bohan standing in the middle of the road, dazed and bleeding. By the time Moore got to the demolished building, six local men were already there, digging among the rubble in the dark, frantically trying to lift the debris with their bare hands, picks and shovels. Sergeant Cannon was able to pinpoint the spot where Ben Thornton was buried and the rescuers began digging for him. They found pieces of his clothing and feared the worst. Ten minutes later, they hauled the detective from the rubble. He was badly hurt but still breathing. When the bomb went off, Thornton had been blown face down and a falling beam had landed over his head. The beam saved his life by creating an air pocket and protecting his head from falling masonry.

At that stage, Cannon knew that Garda Clerkin was dead. He had been blown to pieces. His shattered young body had to be formally identified by his signet-ring. Cannon, Thornton and Bohan eventually recovered from their injuries. Despite extensive surgery Thomas Peters never recovered his sight. He now is blind and almost completely deaf.

Throughout the day, Clerkin's garda colleagues took it in shifts to claw through the wreckage, lifting huge mounds of debris, rock by rock. The only sound that could be heard was the grating of shovels on pulverised stone as they continued their grim task. They stopped automatically each time a black plastic bag was produced to take away a piece of evidence. There were so many plastic bags: in the laneway, in front of the house and behind them. Some of the gardaí were in tears at the sheer horror of it all. One of Clerkin's colleagues, Garda Michael Gillespie, recalled how only a week earlier they had played a round of golf together. Other gardaí had begun combing the fields around the house, and checkpoints had been set up on all roads leading to the area. The Fine Gael Minister for Justice, Patrick Cooney, visited the scene of the explosion and said the killing of a garda proved that the country was indeed in a state of emergency. If it deteriorated further, more new measures would have to be considered, he said. The minister did not spell out what these might include, but his remarks were broadly interpreted to mean one thing — internment.

WITHIN HOURS of the murder, the first wave of arrests began. And within three days, the new Emergency Powers Act swung into action. The first person to be detained under the new legislation was a man named Eamon Hoey. On 19 October, detectives arrested Hoey at Portarlington railway station as he returned to Laois from Dublin and held him for seven days in connection with the Mountmellick bomb. He was released without charge, but was rearrested a fortnight later, at 7.10 p.m. on 5 November. He challenged his detention in the High Court on 11 November. The court declared the second arrest unlawful, as Hoey had been arrested twice for the same crime 'even though the police had acquired further information between the dates of the two arrests'. Eamon Hoey was never charged.

The army would later estimate that the Mountmellick bomb had been 100 pounds in weight and made of gelignite. It was a sophisticated bomb, similar to the one used to murder Christopher Ewart-Biggs three months earlier. Detectives would later have cause to suspect that the same man (not Eamon Hoey) had constructed both bombs. He later fled to the US, where attempts to extradite him failed. He is thought to be still living in the States. Gardaí were also to discover that the Mountmellick bomb had been made in a house located between Tullamore and Clara in County Offaly. But in the immediate aftermath of the Clerkin murder, they had no definite leads. They swooped on six republicans, all male and all from the midlands, and brought them to Portlaoise Garda Station for questioning. The following day, Sunday, they arrested five members of the Irish Republican Socialist Party (IRSP) — the political wing of the newly emerging Irish National Liberation Army (INLA) — as they arrived in Dublin from Belfast. They were brought to the Bridewell Garda Station in Dublin. A large contingent of gardaí was on duty outside the Bridewell as members of the IRSP picketed the station in protest over the use of the new Act.

The Provisional IRA issued a statement denying responsibility for the bomb: 'After investigation, we are satisfied that no member of the Irish Republican Army was in any way involved in the explosion at Mountmellick County Laois in which Garda Michael Clerkin was killed. — P. O'Neill.' The annual Sinn Féin Ard Fheis was due to open in the Mansion House in Dublin on the day Michael Clerkin was murdered. The party moved quickly to distance itself from the bomb. In an interview Sinn Féin's publicity officer, Seán Ó Brádaigh, condemned the killing and described it as an act of sabotage. Neither he, nor anyone else, knew what group was responsible for the County Laois outrage, but he would not regard it as being part of any campaign against the state, he said. Such an attack against the Southern security forces could only be regarded as a 'stab in the back', but it would not nullify his party's opposition to the state of emergency, he added. Despite these denials, there is little doubt that the IRA were responsible for the bomb.

There was a separate meeting in Dublin that weekend of the IRA leadership. At that meeting, the leadership decided that all those charged with membership of the IRA should, in future, recognise the Special Criminal Court and plead not guilty. Up until October 1976, republicans facing the charge had refused to recognise the court. The latest change of tack was a direct reaction to the new legislation, which, as mentioned, upped the sentence for membership from two to seven years. All those held for the Mountmellick bomb were subsequently released without charge.

In Dublin, meanwhile, a presidential crisis was developing over Cearbhall Ó Dálaigh's decision to refer the Emergency Powers Bill to the Supreme Court. Two days after the Mountmellick bomb, the Fine Gael Minister for Defence, Paddy Donegan, called the President a 'thundering disgrace' at an Irish army function at Columb Barracks in Mullingar, County Westmeath. His abusive attack incensed Ó Dálaigh, who interpreted the insult as a slur on the office of President. The Cosgrave government stood by their minister, and in protest, on 22 October, Cearbhall Ó Dálaigh resigned. The Emergency Powers Act went out of operation one year after its enactment and was subsequently removed from the statute-book.

THE MOUNTMELLICK blast occurred against a backdrop of heightened tension between republicans and the gardaí in Portlaoise. There had been several incidents involving Provos and the Special Branch in the town in the run-up to the explosion, culminating in the arrest of three IRA men in the area shortly beforehand. Neither Michael Clerkin nor any of the other gardaí who responded to the call were the intended targets of the bomb. It was meant for another plain-clothes officer in Portlaoise against whom certain Provos had a grudge. The Provos who planted it had expected that this detective would respond to the phone warning and be lured to his death. When contacted by this author, this officer would neither confirm nor deny suggestions that he was the intended victim, but it did not come as a complete surprise to him.

Michael Clerkin was known personally to some of the republican inmates in Portlaoise. Before the outbreak of the Troubles he had taught one of them to swim in his home town of Monaghan. His killing, and the blinding of Thomas Peters, did not go down well within certain sections of the IRA and those responsible for the outrage were subsequently isolated. There are some suggestions that Mountmellick was a 'solo run', although others reject this and say the bombing had to have been sanctioned.

The horrific nature of Michael Clerkin's death stunned his colleagues, many of whom were friends of the young garda. 'I remember that night leaving the station with him,' recalled Paddy Egan, who is now retired:

> I offered to do the shift to let him out with the girlfriend

but he said, no problem, he'd do it. Then, when I heard at about 1.30 that night that he'd been in an explosion … it was desperate. He was a very gentle fellow, Michael. I remember the time he was only starting out and he had stopped someone for a minor offence. When he was making out the summons he came to me and asked if the guy would be able to pay the fine. That's the kind of lad he was.

In Portarlington, Clerkin had been very involved in local youth and swimming clubs. He had also worked alongside Jim Cannon in trying to set up non-alcohol discos for teenagers: 'He was very popular here, and to see him dying like that … I knew when we found Ben Thornton that Michael was dead. He couldn't have survived it. It's a miracle that Ben Thornton was pulled out alive. Michael hadn't a chance. He stepped right on the bomb.'

MICHAEL CLERKIN was the fourth garda to die violently in six years. At twenty-four, he would not have known the Garda Síochána as it was in quieter, less troubled times, as many of his older colleagues did. When he was killed, Jack Marrinan of the Garda Representative Association wondered if the time had come to arm the gardaí and revive the death penalty:

With four of our members slain since the beginning of the disturbances in Northern Ireland, with many more injured and with increasingly frequent use of firearms and explosives against our members, we must stop and take stock of the situation … Capital punishment remains on the statute-books. If the cold-blooded, deliberate, calculated murder of members of the Garda Síochána were to be a feature of the troubles in this country, the force would not be able to carry on without it.

The people of Monaghan town were stunned by the murder of Michael Clerkin. Before joining the gardaí he had worked in the footwear industry in Monaghan, where his father, Patrick, had a shoe shop. He had attended the Christian Brothers school in Monaghan up to Leaving Cert. The Clerkins were a well-known family and very well liked. There were seven in the family, Margaret, Peter, Assumpta, Michael, Dolores, Marie and Pádraig. Pádraig, who now works in the Monaghan Museum, was just seventeen when his brother was killed. He answered the door at 3 a.m. and found Sergeant Holland standing there with a local doctor: 'He first told me Michael had been in an accident; then he told me he'd been killed. Then the doctor came in. My mother had to be sedated; Michael was the light of her life. He had a way about him and it was reciprocated by Mam.' Pádraig, Peter and Paddy Duffy, a brother-in-law, travelled to Portlaoise to identify the young garda's body. When they arrived, they were not allowed to see him: 'He was identified by his ring: they wouldn't let us in to see him,' said Pádraig. 'It's only afterwards you realise that he wasn't in a fit state to be seen.'

Peter, the eldest of the Clerkin brothers, recalls Michael wanting to be a guard and walking around the town with Garda Denis Connolly when he was a youngster. Peter also remembers that Michael had to change his ways a little to fulfil his ambition: 'At the first interview he was told to get his hair cut; he was the most unlikely looking potential guard you ever saw … He had a devilish sense of humour but he had a compassion about him. But he did become more conservative in the guards; he took his job very seriously.'

A week after his death, Michael Clerkin's long-awaited transfer came through; it had been in the post at the time of his murder. He was to have been transferred to Trim, a move that would have pleased him. Referring to his brother's time in secondment at Portlaoise, Assumpta Duffy said 'He hated working in the prison. Michael hadn't a political bone in his body and he couldn't wait to get out of Portlaoise. He hated that aspect of the job.' Ten days before he was killed, he had received a letter from his mother, Mary, in which she referred to his unhappiness during his time at Portlaoise and his disappointment at the prospect of returning there:

> So sorry I missed you when you phoned on Thursday night. Dad and Peter were saying that you heard a rumour that you were to go into the prison full time. I am sure you were disappointed when you heard that. Hope it does not come off and that you will be able to do something about it … Will you be home on Friday? Dolores rang on Sunday night. She is in Greece by now I hope … Don't wait to write any more now, hoping all goes well for you and that we will see you at the weekend.
>
> Love Mam, Dad, Peter and Pádraig

Dolores was on her way back from holiday in Greece when she heard that her brother had been killed: 'I was flying home from Athens to Manchester when a policeman came on the plane and told me that Michael had been killed. Someone gave up their seat to allow me to fly back to Dublin because the funeral was being held up until I got back.'

It rained on the day of the funeral. For an hour, the funeral cortège moved through the packed, silent streets of Portlaoise.

Then it picked up speed for the journey to Monaghan, where more than two thousand of the young garda's neighbours and friends were waiting on its arrival. For Michael Clerkin's girlfriend, Betty Cooper, it was a particularly harrowing day. They had planned to get engaged at Christmas. The writer Evelyn Conlon was also among the mourners; she and Michael had been childhood friends. As a young poet in Australia in 1973, Conlon had written a poem for him: 'Click Clerkin'. Almost hidden among the thousands of mourners crowding around the graveside at Latlurcan Cemetery was the dead garda's colleague Gerry Bohan, who bore the scars of the explosion on his face. Monaghan had not seen scenes like it since May 1974, when it had suffered its own bombing at the hands of loyalist paramilitaries. The garda chaplain, Fr Clarence Daly, said it was in trying to combat such atrocities that Michael Clerkin died: 'Michael lived a short life, but he lived a good life, and that is ultimately what matters.'

'Michael had a very good manner,' recalls his sister Dolores. 'When he'd come home, he'd slip a few pounds into my mother's purse. He'd come home every four to six weeks and he'd take Mam and Dad on trips.' Mary Clerkin died of cancer a few months after her son was killed. Assumpta feels her brother's death accelerated her mother's illness. 'She was devastated; she never got over it. And because she got sick so quickly after Michael died all our concentration was on her.' Peter Clerkin recalls the repressed pain of his brother's death: 'When I look back, I was not allowed to cry because I was the eldest boy, but I wanted to cry, he was my brother. I remember coming back with the remains, Assumpta's husband, Paddy, was driving and we were coming through a checkpoint and having to convince the guards that we were family.'

Dolores, who at the time was a nurse at Grangegorman psychiatric hospital in Dublin, found the state funeral hard to deal with: 'The funeral was very public. I resented that my mother's grief was so public because she was a very dignified woman, she was very reserved. It was awfully hard on her.' Marie Clerkin was in London and Margaret in Dublin when they heard the news of their brother's death. 'There was just a complete state of shock for about a week. We were totally numb,' said Margaret. 'After that it begins to sink in slowly and it's only then it hits you.'

Patrick Clerkin had been a supporter of Fianna Fáil and had actively canvassed for the party, but at that time his sons and daughters were not aware of party politics. 'In a small town, everyone mixes. You are not aware, growing up, of social and political differences; they come later,' said Dolores. 'His murder was taken with utter disgust in Monaghan, by everybody.'

The Clerkins have never received an official account of their brother's death, to which they feel they are entitled. 'All we got was word of mouth,' said Dolores. 'And because we never heard anything official, we feel that the final chapter in Michael's life has not been written. Looking back now, we should have been more proactive, but our father was very fatalistic in a way, very resigned, no bitterness. We don't have either, but we should not have let it lie the way we did. But we fully expected that because Michael was a guard killed in the line of duty something would have been done to bring someone to justice.'

In 1984, his colleagues in Portarlington unveiled a plaque in his honour, but, unlike many other gardaí killed in the line of duty, Michael Clerkin was not awarded the Scott medal posthumously. During the celebrations to mark the seventy-fifth anniversary of the establishment of the Garda Síochána in 1997, a local sergeant in Monaghan called to Peter Clerkin looking for memorabilia belonging to Michael. As a teenager in Monaghan, Michael had been very involved in athletics, particularly the long jump and cross-country running. Peter pulled out some of Michael's medals: 'I gave them to him and then he said "What about the Scott medal?" I said "What medal? Michael never got one." The sergeant was amazed.'

Sometime during 2000, the family wrote to the Garda Commissioner, Pat Byrne, seeking information about their brother's murder. In August 2000, the Garda Commissioner's office replied to the Clerkins' letter: 'Please be assured that the memory of Michael and the others who paid the ultimate sacrifice in the service of their country will not be forgotten.'

'The reply didn't address the issues we raised,' said Dolores. 'There were two issues. The first was we never had any official explanation surrounding Michael's death; all we got was hearsay. The second was we feel that he never got due recognition; we feel that part of his life story isn't closed, we never had closure.'

5

Detective Garda John Morley and Garda Henry Byrne

❧❧❧

Shortly after lunchtime on a sunny Monday afternoon, a blue Ford Cortina car coasted to a stop outside the Bank of Ireland at Ballaghaderreen, a small town in County Roscommon. It was 7 July 1980. The bank's assistant manager, Thomas Gallagher, was at the counter. It was his first day in the Ballaghaderreen branch on transfer from Claremorris, County Mayo. Two masked and armed men jumped out of the Cortina and ran into the bank, while a third stayed outside on Main Street. Once inside the bank, the two men fanned out and fired a shot at the ceiling with a long barrelled gun. 'Everybody get down,' shouted one of the raiders, a tall, slim man. 'If anyone moves kill them,' he said to his accomplice. 'Keep cool,' cautioned the second raider in a low, calm voice.

The first raider went under the counter leaf, past Thomas Gallagher towards the bank's acting manager, Fintan Donnelly. 'Open this,' he ordered, pointing to the strongroom where the safes were held. There was plenty of cash in the safes: a couple of days earlier, the cash centre at Sligo had delivered £56,000 to the Ballaghaderreen branch. Donnelly took the keys from a grid and then went to get a second set. He opened the door to the strongroom and the raider pushed the manager inside. He had a gun in his right hand and a bag in the other. 'Fill it,' he shouted, shoving the bag at him. 'It's better to lose money than have someone killed.' The raider noticed another drawer. 'Open it,' he said. Donnelly had no keys and told him so. 'I'll take your word for it.' He nodded towards the second safe and asked what was in it. Just coin, said the manager, and the raider left the strongroom.

Donnelly went out to the main floor where the customers were lying on the floor, cowering. Meanwhile, one of the gunmen had vaulted the counter and began scooping up cash. Frank McAnena, a nearby shopkeeper, was serving customers when someone came in and said there was something up at the bank. McAnena went out to check and he saw the third raider keeping watch outside the branch. The town was quiet; there was just a man with a gun standing there looking up and down the near-deserted street. It was like a scene from the Wild West, McAnena said later.

Outside, the Ballaghaderreen patrol car was pulling up about twenty yards from the bank. Garda Brendan Gilmore and Garda Brendan Walsh had been on routine patrol when a passing motorist told them that the bank was being held up. 'Go to the garda station and report it,' said Walsh, while turning the squad car and heading for Main Street. The gardaí had intended driving around the branch, leaving the car and 'sneaking up' on the raiders. They were starting to get out when the lookout man spotted them. He caught Walsh by the hand and put a gun to his head: 'Get out of the car and don't try anything.' The gunman ripped the speaker from the patrol car, threw it on the ground and forced the gardaí to the ground beside it. Inside, the raiders had just finished scooping up whatever cash they could get their hands on. It was all over in minutes. They jumped back into the car, threw the bag of cash onto the back seat, gunned the engine and sped down Main Street, cheering. They had escaped with £41,000.

Garda P.J. Kilcullen was in Ballaghaderreen Garda Station when he noticed the Cortina moving off. When it came to the top of the town he saw a man in the passenger seat with his hand out the window holding a shotgun. The Cortina drove back down the town again, past the garda station, then made a U-turn and headed for the main Dublin road. Garda units at Castlerea had now been alerted to the armed bank robbery and were speeding towards Ballaghaderreen. Garda Henry Byrne had been rostered for day shifts that week and was due to finish at 2 p.m. He was working in Castlerea on the 'town beat' when the call came through. He hopped into one of the patrol cars with gardaí Derek O'Kelly and Mick O'Malley. There was one armed officer in the car, Detective Garda John Morley.

Morley had been at a funeral that morning. After the funeral he went home to Knock Row for his lunch and was back in Castlerea Garda Station at 2 p.m., around the time the alarm was raised. The four gardaí were speeding towards the scene of the robbery when a message came over the garda radio that the raiders had been spotted turning off onto a secondary road towards Frenchpark. They had torched the blue Cortina and had switched to a white one, which they had hidden near Ballaghaderreen. A twelve-year-old girl, Mary Callaghan, had gone to a friend's house that day and was standing beside the road near Lisacul when two cars passed her at high speed, heading for Shannon's Cross. She heard a screech of brakes followed by gunshots. Garda Derek O'Kelly was driving the patrol car. He reduced speed while turning a sharp bend at Shannon's Cross. As he was pressing down on the accelerator again, he saw the white Cortina bearing down from the Moyne direction.

The getaway car smashed into the patrol car, on the right front side. The left door of the Cortina opened and a tall, hooded man in combat jacket got out. He was holding a shotgun in his right hand. He pointed the gun at O'Kelly's head and the garda ducked under the steering wheel. Without any warning, the gunman opened fire on the men inside the patrol car. Another gunman fired a burst of shots from a revolver into the patrol car, shattering the front windscreen and rear windows. Glass was flying everywhere. The volley of bullets hit Garda Henry Byrne, who was sitting on the back seat. The gunmen tried to reverse back, but forgot to close the door and it got jammed in a telegraph pole. They abandoned the car and headed for the open fields. One ran towards Frenchpark and the others headed in the direction of Castlerea. Detective Morley, armed with an Uzi sub-machine-gun, ran after them. 'Hold it,' he shouted at them. They kept on running.

Henry Byrne was lying in the back of the patrol car beside the door, dying from a bullet wound to the back of the head. Garda Mick O'Malley called Byrne's name but there was no response. He kneeled beside him and whispered a prayer into his ear. There was a car registration number, VLI 168, scribbled in biro on Byrne's left palm. His garda cap was still where he had left it, on the back rest of the patrol car.

The fleeing gunmen came out onto the road where they had the protection of a small bridge. Detective Morley stopped running and levelled his sub-machine-gun at them. At that moment a cyclist appeared on the scene. 'Get down,' Morley shouted. A single shot rang out and the detective collapsed in a pool of blood on the ground beside a ditch, tumbling backwards as he fell. He was bleeding from a leg wound. In the few moments it took O'Kelly and O'Malley to reach him, his beige slacks had become saturated with blood. Before he fell, Morley had managed to let off a round from his machine-gun. He was rolling from side to side in pain. He told O'Kelly that he felt cold. The garda urged him to hang in there; help was on its way and he would pull through. Detective Morley must have known otherwise: 'Say goodbye to my wife and kids for me,' he whispered to his colleague.

Gardaí flagged down a passing motorist and asked him to bring Morley to Roscommon Hospital. There was no time to wait for an ambulance: the detective was dying. Garda Henry Byrne appeared to be dead. Garda P.J. Kilcullen, who was now on the scene, accompanied Byrne's body to Roscommon Hospital. When he arrived, he saw John Morley's body lying on a slab in the morgue. He had died on the way to hospital. The bullet had severed the main artery in his left leg and he had bled to death. 'It was an awful shock to see his body there,' Kilcullen said. It was only at that moment that he realised that Detective Morley had been shot dead along with Henry Byrne.

THAT AFTERNOON, Frances Morley was at home in Knock Row minding her three children, Shane, aged eleven, Gillian, nine, and the youngest, Gordon, aged four. In the morning, she had attended the same funeral as her husband. John Morley, a prominent GAA footballer, had organised the guard of honour at the funeral of Mrs Burke, the mother of a garda colleague, Danny Burke. 'I can still see him kneeling there at the back of the church,' recalls Frances Morley, 'wearing a brown jacket and beige slacks. We went to the grave and I went home to put the dinner on. John had a bit to eat after the funeral and then he went back to the station.'

Less than an hour after he had left the house, one of the children ran in from the garden where they were playing tennis: 'Mum, Auntie Monica wants you.' Monica, John Morley's sister, lived just down the road. Frances picked up Gordon and went down to see what was up. When she got there, Monica's husband, J.J. McFadden, said there had been a phone call about 'some kind of accident, or bank robbery' and that somebody had been hurt. The phone message had been a bit jumbled. It was around 2.50 p.m. The gardaí eventually came up to Frances Morley's house. They told her that Henry Byrne had been killed instantly and that John had got out of the patrol car to run after the gunmen: 'They did not say much but I knew it was serious. I remember having Gordon in my arms, pacing up and down, fearing the worst. I came out to the door. Dr Greg Kelly was standing there. He just looked at me and said "This is the hardest thing I have ever done." I knew then that John was dead.'

Gillian had been down at the local swimming pool when neighbours went to fetch her. They told her she 'had to be good for her mam'. 'We went to the morgue in Roscommon; the children did see him at some stage. Everything was so unreal. It was just like it was happening to someone else. I remember thinking "This could not be happening to us."'

AT SHANNON'S Cross, all available squad cars were speeding towards the scene of the murders. It was the first time since the foundation of the state that two gardaí had been killed together after a bank robbery. When word of the tragedy filtered through to Ballaghaderreen, the townspeople could hardly take in the enormity of what had just happened in their midst. Even hardened detectives were shocked that the lives of two young colleagues had been wiped out in a flash. The gunmen were trying desperately to escape. After they shot Morley, they stopped a Volkswagen and trailer being driven by Michael Kneafsey, whose son, Thomas, was a passenger in the car. Two of the gunmen went to either side of Kneafsey's car and pulled father and son from the car. As Michael grappled with one gunman a shot rang out and his son dived onto the grass, uninjured but terrified.

The gunmen took the trailer off the Volkswagen, jumped into the car and sped off in the direction of Loughglinn. It was only then that Michael Kneafsey saw a man lying on the ground; he recognised John Morley, as he had seen the detective playing football for Mayo 'many a time'. At that stage, Morley was still conscious but his face was deathly white. The Kneafseys walked further up the road and saw another man lying on the ground covered with a blanket. It was Henry Byrne.

The first break in the case came early that afternoon. Sligo detective Allo Farragher got information that one of the gunmen had been spotted driving towards a small wood close to Cloonfad, a townland in County Roscommon. When the gardaí got there, locals directed them to a narrow little road, leading to the wood. There was just one entrance and exit but inside was a maze of small tracks and pathways. The gardaí had just turned onto a narrow pathway when they saw a man sitting on a wall in front of a small house. There was blood on his clothes and chest and he appeared to be injured. When he saw the gardaí approaching, he stood up and put his hands in the air. He identified himself as Colm O'Shea, from Sunday's Well in Cork. He told them that he had been shot.

Gardaí arrested the twenty-eight-year-old man under section 30 of the Offences Against the State Act and then arranged for him to be taken to Galway Regional Hospital for treatment for gunshot wounds. In a dramatic midnight sitting that night, the High Court in Dublin ruled that, contrary to O'Shea's claims, he was legally in custody and could be charged before the Special Criminal Court when deemed medically fit. This was not the first time O'Shea found himself on the wrong side of the law. In the 1970s, he had been jailed for six years for robbing the Pye electronics factory in Dundrum in Dublin. He was an extreme left-winger and had connections with the Irish Republican Socialist Party and the Communist Party.

Checkpoints had been set up all over the mid-west as far south as Clare. The following day, at about 10 p.m., Garda Tom Lynch was at a checkpoint just outside Frenchpark on the road to Ballaghaderreen when a local man approached him with a piece of information that turned out to be crucial. While drinking in the Sheepmore Way bar, this local man had noticed a stranger come in and disappear shortly afterwards. Something about him aroused suspicions. The local man gave Lynch a brief description of him.

The next morning, at about 9 a.m., Lynch saw a man walking in the direction of the checkpoint who seemed to fit the description. He was about one hundred yards from the checkpoint when he suddenly turned and began walking in the opposite direction. The man went into Fleming's Garage and stood against a car with his hands in his pocket. His hair was dishevelled, his face was dirty and there were scratches and dried blood on the back of his hands. He was very tired looking. He was Patrick McCann, a thirty-four-year-old man from Dungarvan in County Waterford with an address in Leeson Park in Dublin. Like O'Shea, he had been involved with the Communist Party and was also known to the gardaí. In 1972, he had been sentenced to eighteen months for possession of firearms.

Gardaí took McCann into custody under section 30. They removed his clothes and placed him in a cell in Frenchpark Garda Station. (McCann would later complain that he had been left naked in the cell for two hours.) The prisoner was questioned about the Ballaghaderreen robbery and the killing of two gardaí at Shannon's Cross. He knew nothing about any robbery or any killings: 'I didn't rob the bank, I shot no one,' he replied. He asked for a drink of water, but when the glass was produced he refused to drink from it until two officers had tasted it first. O'Shea and McCann were taken to the Special Criminal Court in Dublin at midnight on 10 July and charged with the capital murder of Garda Henry Byrne, the robbery of £41,000 from the Bank of Ireland and firearms offences.

Nine days later, gardaí arrested a man at Ballybane Cottage in Galway. They knocked on the door, but when there was no reply they got in through the window. While searching the upstairs of the house they found a man hiding in an alcove. When detectives asked him his name he replied 'Pringle'. When asked where he was from he replied 'Dublin'. He was Peter Pringle, a forty-two-year-old fisherman with an address at Ringsend in Dublin. He too was known to the gardaí: in the late 1950s, he was one of a large number of people interned on suspicion of IRA membership and was sentenced to three months for failing to account for his movements. The gardaí had put his Scandinavian girlfriend, Eva Curtin, under surveillance and she had unwittingly led them to Ballybane Cottage. After being taken under section 30 to Eglinton Street Garda Station in Galway, he was charged with capital murder and remanded for trial the following October.

JOHN MORLEY and Henry Byrne were buried side by side on a hillside graveyard overlooking Knock in County Mayo. They had both been reared in the same parish — Byrne in Knock and Morley in Faughill, a village between Knock and Kiltimagh. Henry Byrne was twenty-nine years old. He was married with two young sons and his wife, Anne, was pregnant with their third child. He had been a garda for eight years and had been stationed in Mullingar, Multifarnham, Granard and Carlow before moving to Castlerea.

At thirty-eight, John Morley was the youngest of eight children, whose parents were both dead. His mother had died when he was just two years old, his father in 1970. The detective was very well known in sporting and youth circles in Ballaghaderreen, but probably best known for his footballing skills, playing for Mayo. He was captain of the Mayo team that won the National Football League title in 1970. 'He was very easy going, John. He enjoyed people and got on well with them,' recalls his widow, Frances. The couple had met when she was just seventeen and studying for the Leaving Cert. in Collooney, County Sligo. He was just two years older and was working in Gowna Industries in Collooney as a rep. It was his first job. After she left school she joined the civil service, and in 1964, John joined the gardaí. Four years later, they married. John Morley's first posting as a garda was in Kilmainham in Dublin, after which he was stationed in Ballaghaderreen and Roscommon before moving to Castlerea. 'He came on promotion to Castlerea in 1978 and he liked it there,' said Frances:

> When John was killed, there were so many people around and then all of a sudden you're on your own. At the time I couldn't think straight. I never even thought of where we were going to bury him. Someone asked where did we want him buried. Before I had a chance to answer, Shane said 'Knock'. So that's what we did. Looking back though, everything was done the way the authorities wanted it; with a state funeral everything is taken out of your hands. After the funeral, when it sinks in, you get angry, but my biggest anger was with John, for dying and leaving us alone. You can be bitter and resentful but life is hard enough without that. I've tried to rear the children without bitterness, because it would only end up destroying the kids and me.

Gillian Morley was perhaps the closest to her father; her favourite occupation as a youngster was kicking ball with her Dad:

> My last memory of Dad was sitting on his knee that day, before he went back to the station. We were sitting at the table and I was pulling his ears and putting my thumb in his mouth: I used to do that all the time. I used to call to the garda station on my way home from school and give him in my schoolbag and say 'Dad, will you bring that home for me?' It hits you most on happy occasions, family times. And he's not here to share them.

Gillian, a nurse, is married to a garda in Galway and they have two young children, Amy and Cathal. John would have loved them, reflects Frances:

> We're a very close family and that's what keeps us going. Confirmation, Communion, they were the hardest times. But out of every evil comes a good. The grandchildren are here now and it's a great pity he's not here to see them. John always used to say 'When the kids grow up, we'll still be here.' As years go by, life takes a whole new meaning; you learn to cope. After he died it was hard to go out as a single person; it was difficult, but life goes on; it's never the same, but you just get on with it.

FRANCES MORLEY decided not to attend the trial when it opened in the Special Criminal Court in October 1980. It was her way of shutting it out, she said. Colm O'Shea, Patrick McCann and Peter Pringle had all pleaded not guilty to the capital murder of Garda Henry Byrne. (None was charged with the murder of Detective John Morley. It was felt at the time that a conviction for capital murder would be more likely in respect of the killing of Garda Byrne. As he was in uniform when he was shot, the killers could have been in no doubt that Byrne was a garda.) During the trial, statements allegedly made by all three were produced in evidence but were contested bitterly by their lawyers. Forensic and circumstantial evidence was another matter. The forensic evidence against O'Shea and McCann was to prove overwhelming. Footprints found on the counter of the Bank of Ireland were shown to have matched diamond-shaped prints from O'Shea's size-ten runners. The 'worn areas' and defects on his runners corresponded with those on the counter. A head hair lifted from the Cortina matched O'Shea's hair. In the opinion of the state forensic witness, it was a 'one in four thousand' match. Four small fragments of dark red paint found in O'Shea's pockets were proven to be the same as those found in the rear seat of the Cortina abandoned by the gang at Shannon's Cross. Forensic scientists had compared the impression taken from a piece of earth near the scene of the shooting with Patrick McCann's Farrah trousers and found they matched exactly. The impression of the heel of his wellington boot also matched.

On Thursday, 27 November 1980, after six hours of deliberation, the three judges found the accused men guilty as charged. There was only one sentence the court could pass: death by hanging. As the three were taken down to the cells below, O'Shea gave a clenched fist salute. 'Good luck, Colm,' shouted a supporter. What appeared to be a flower was thrown down from the public gallery, but it was caught by a garda. The death sentence was later commuted to one of forty years' imprisonment, which, fifteen years later, was to have particular resonance in Peter Pringle's case.

Of all things, it was a chance nosebleed that led to Peter Pringle's reprieve in May 1995. Evidence of the existence of a bloodstained tissue used to stem the flow of blood from Pringle's nose during detention had been given in court during the 1980 trial. It provided a possible link between him and the bloodstains found in the getaway car. The reference to the nosebleed was entered in a garda's notebook but no forensic analysis was carried out due to the insufficient amount of blood available on the tissue. The notebook entry stated that the tissue had been handed to another garda. This second garda denied it. The conflict between the two gardaí, which was not raised at the

1980 trial, introduced a reasonable doubt concerning Pringle's conviction. The Court of Criminal Appeal found that this conflict between the two gardaí amounted to new evidence and ordered a retrial. On 17 May, Pringle was granted bail of £60,000 while awaiting the retrial, which never went ahead. A fortnight later, in a one-minute hearing, the Special Criminal Court struck out all charges against him. Peter Pringle, grey-haired and fifteen years older, was a free man, innocent of all charges. After the hearing, he said he would 'walk the mountains and walk by the sea'.

Frances Morley heard about Pringle's imminent release from an RTÉ reporter, Ciarán Mullooly:

> He rang us five minutes before the main evening news and asked had we heard about Peter Pringle. I told him I knew nothing about it. That was the biggest knock; we should have been told by the authorities, but we weren't. About ten days later, I was in the departure lounge in Dublin Airport and I happened to turn around and he was there behind me. I recognised him straight away. I have seen him since, driving around Galway: I have been at one bank machine while he was at another. I would rather not see him but I have no bitterness towards him. You would not like to think an innocent man was in jail. I would like to think a person is innocent until proven guilty.

It has taken Frances Morley twenty years to allow her feelings to reach the surface and accept things as they are:

> Those other two guys, well they've served twenty years so far. I was quite satisfied with the verdict. I'm sure those

men did not go out that day to kill anyone; they probably thought they'd rob the bank and get away with it. But there again it was planned and they were carrying guns and were prepared for any eventuality. I am looking at things differently than I would have years ago. Then you think, so many guards have been killed since John and Henry and you begin to question the whole thing again, after each killing. We're only human after all. But at least in our case, we've had closure. Some of the other families haven't had that, and you do need closure.

Neither Colm O'Shea nor Patrick McCann qualified for early release under the terms of the Good Friday Agreement. In March 2001, O'Shea took a High Court case challenging the state's failure to qualify him for early release. The case is due to be heard in 2002.

6

Detective Garda
James Quaid

In January 1972, seven men imprisoned on a ship anchored in a corner of Belfast Lough got together to form an escape plan. They had already decided to make a break for freedom; all they needed to discuss now were the ways and means. The men were internees aboard the *Maidstone*, a rusty old troop-ship that had been pressed into action when the Northern Ireland Prime Minister, Brian Faulkner, introduced internment on 9 August 1971, under the North's Special Powers Act. In immediate, simultaneous dawn swoops across the North, three thousand British troops arrested hundreds of nationalists, many of whom were listed on out-of-date RUC Special Branch files. Internment — locking people up without trial — was a draconian, knee-jerk reaction to the Provisional IRA's armed campaign, which had been well under way since the start of 1971. Between January and August of that year, the Provisionals carried out more than three hundred explosions and three hundred and twenty shooting incidents. During that time, loyalist mobs went on the rampage burning nationalists out of their homes, razing entire streets. There was widespread rioting throughout the North.

Politically, internment was a disaster. In practical terms it had been ill thought out, with little consideration as to where the hundreds of internees were to be held. Bars were hurriedly bolted onto the *Maidstone*'s portholes and it was quickly turned into a floating prison, just as the first group of internees were being rounded up. One of them was Peter Rogers, a twenty-seven-year-old busman from Slemish Way, Andersonstown, in west Belfast.

Rogers was a key figure in the escape, which involved swimming half a mile through the icy waters of the Musgrave Channel towards the pier in Belfast Lough. He and another six men had been hand-picked for the escape. They arranged for hacksaws to be smuggled on board, and on the night of 17 January, they sawed the bars off the portholes, crawled through, slid down the hawser and plunged into the water. They had rubbed butter onto their bodies to protect against the cold, put socks on their hands and feet for protection against the metal hawser, and blacked themselves out with boot polish to avoid being spotted by the *Maidstone*'s arc lights.

All seven made it safely to shore. When they reached dry land they hijacked a bus and Rogers took over the wheel. He drove through the dock gates just before the alarm was raised and reached the Markets area of the city with relative ease. Rogers knew the roads like the back of his hand. From there, they made it safely to Dublin, where the 'Magnificent Seven', as they were now being called in the republican heartlands, held a triumphant press conference with IRA leaders Seán Mac Stiofáin and Joe Cahill. Peter Rogers stayed in Dublin for a while. Then he headed for County Wexford.

DETECTIVE GARDA James Quaid had been stationed in Wexford since 1958, the year he joined the gardaí. In 1980 he was forty-two years old and married with four children aged from eight to eighteen. Quaid, from Ballinakill, Castlemahon, in Limerick, had been an all-Ireland hurler. He had played for Limerick and Wexford, and in 1960 won an all-Ireland senior hurling medal with Wexford. One of Quaid's detective duties was to monitor the movements of known republicans. One of them was Peter Rogers.

After Rogers arrived from Dublin he moved to Rosslare, where he landed a job with the Irish Continental Line ferry the *St Patrick* on the Rosslare to Le Harve route. In March 1977, he married a woman from Enniscorthy and the couple went to live in a mobile home at Knocktown, in Duncormick, County Wexford. Three years later, his wife, Deirdre, gave birth to a baby boy, Eamonn. At some point, the Belfast man had a row with the captain of the *St Patrick* and left the ferry job. During all of his time in Wexford, Peter Rogers was active in Provisional IRA and Sinn Féin circles. During the H-Block blanket protest and the first IRA hunger strike campaign in 1980, Rogers was active in drumming up support for the prisoners' cause. Detective James Quaid knew Peter Rogers well. They were on first name terms with each other. On numerous occasions, detectives had taken Rogers in for questioning about paramilitary activities. He was a very quiet man and seldom lost his cool. After he left Irish Continental Line, the Belfast man started his own greengrocery business, travelling all over the county. He would buy vegetables from local growers and sell them in Wexford town. At the same time, Peter Rogers was also transporting firearms, explosives and ammunition for the Provos.

On Monday, 13 October 1980, two banks were held up in Callan, County Kilkenny. Armed and masked men escaped with more than £10,000 from the Allied Irish Bank and the Bank of

Ireland. By any standards, they were audacious raids: soldiers driving a petrol tanker (the country was in the throes of a petrol crisis at the time) and their garda escort were held at gunpoint while the banks were robbed by raiders carrying sub-machine-guns. The gang robbed the Bank of Ireland branch first, then re-emerged, jumped into a red Ford Escort car and reversed back one hundred yards to the Allied Irish Banks, where they stole £3,500 before returning to collect an accomplice who had been holding the gardaí prisoner. A garda car parked across the road from the banks had its radio ripped out. The gang escaped with the cash.

Detective Quaid and his colleague Detective Garda Donal Lyttleton had been on duty that day and were due to finish at 2.00 p.m., but because of the raids there was plenty of overtime going. Quaid and Lyttleton volunteered to do extra hours, and the two were among scores of gardaí operating roadblocks throughout Kilkenny, Carlow and Wexford and checking out the usual suspects. They decided to check out Peter Rogers. They visited his mobile home twice that day, but he was not there. They then decided to leave it until the following morning. At around 10.30 p.m., Donal Lyttleton was driving the unmarked patrol car through Cleariestown, a townland some thirty miles away from the scene of the bank raids. Quaid was in the front passenger seat. They were travelling along a lonely by-road halfway between Wexford town and Duncannon, near Ballinconnick quarry, when Quaid spotted Rogers' blue Ford Transit van coming towards them on the dark road. The patrol car flagged him down.

Because the Belfast man was well known to both detectives and they were on friendly enough terms, Lyttleton left his gun on the dashboard of the patrol car when he got out to speak to

Rogers. The detectives asked him to open the back of the van. Inside the Transit van was a small arsenal, including eighty-three pounds of Frangex explosives (a type of gelignite), electronic detonators, four guns, decoders, mercury switches and delay-action units for use with primed bombs. Quaid was searching the van when Rogers reached for his gun. It had been hidden between the front seats of the van and was loaded and ready for use.

The Belfast man ordered the two detectives out of the van and into the nearby quarry at gunpoint, firing a shot over their heads. He asked the detectives to let him go — that way 'no one would get hurt'. Quaid responded by pulling out his own gun and ordering Rogers to give himself up. When he refused, Quaid opened fire. Almost simultaneously, Rogers let off a shot from his nine-millimetre handgun. Quaid's first shot passed close to Rogers; another punctured the rear wheel of the van. A short but intense gun battle erupted, during which Quaid fired four shots into Rogers' lower left leg. The Belfast man aimed at Quaid's upper body, hitting him in the lower stomach. The detective lurched backwards and fell to the ground in a crumpled heap. One of the shots had severed the main artery in the detective's leg, causing profuse bleeding. In all, a total of ten shots were fired, six by Quaid and four by Rogers.

Donal Lyttleton, unable to get back to the patrol car to retrieve his weapon, took cover when the shooting started. Helpless without his gun, he none the less made his way across the fields and raised the alarm. Tragically, however, James Quaid was fatally wounded and bled to death within fifteen minutes. Rogers left him lying on the ground, dying. He attempted to escape in the van but when he tried to drive away, he realised the wheel had been punctured by a bullet. He managed to drive for about half a mile, before pulling into a local farmer's yard and stealing an Opel Kadett, in which he drove to Wexford town. He went straight to a friend's house, but he did not tell this man what had happened at Cleariestown less than an hour before. The friend later heard on the news that a garda had been shot. He looked at Rogers' wounds, put two and two together and advised Rogers to give himself up to the gardaí.

PETER ROGERS arrived at Wexford Garda Station with a local priest in the early hours of Tuesday morning. He had to be helped into the interview room. Detective Edward Daly, whom he had known for some time, was there.

'Do you realise the man you just killed had a wife and young family?' Daly asked.

'I begged those two men ...' said Rogers, his voice trailing off.

He buried his head in his hands. Minutes later, he came face to face with Detective Donal Lyttleton. During a short and terse conversation, Lyttleton told the Belfast man that he did not hate him; all he felt towards him was pity. 'It is you who will have to live with this in your heart and in your mind forever,' he said, turning to leave the room.

Later that night, Wexford Garda Station was turned into an impromptu court. Gardaí brought Peter Rogers up from the holding cell to another room where a special sitting of the District Court was being held. There, before a local Peace Commissioner, James Byrne, Rogers was charged with the common law murder of Detective James Quaid at Cleariestown. It was a brief, tense hearing. Shortly afterwards, Rogers was whisked away to Wexford County Hospital for treatment for the bullet wounds in his leg, which had become infected.

Reporters in Wexford had not been informed that the special court sitting was to take place. But at a hurriedly convened press conference soon afterwards, Superintendent Noel Anderson informed them of recent developments. The following morning, the Wexford State Solicitor, Jack McEvoy, told Wexford District Court, that the wrong charge had been laid against Rogers: he had been charged incorrectly with murder contrary to common law, instead of the statutory offence of capital murder. The original charge would now have to be withdrawn. At this stage, Rogers was still in Wexford County Hospital under armed guard. James Quaid's body was lying in the morgue at the same hospital. Rogers' solicitor, maintaining that the court had no jurisdiction to hear the case, withdrew from the courtroom. It was now clear that the Belfast man was going to have to be released.

The gardaí were in a quandary. At Wexford courthouse, Superintendent Anderson told the clatter of reporters gathered outside that 'The man in the county hospital is the man we want in connection with the murder.' He also said that there was no connection between the Callan bank raids and the murder of Detective James Quaid. Rogers had not heard about the raids on the Monday, the day he had decided to shift the explosives. If he had, he would almost certainly have not attempted to remove them from the arms dump, as he knew only too well that as soon as any bank robbery took place, he was one of the first suspects to be rounded up.

On Wednesday afternoon, a row blew up in the Dáil over the mistake that had led to the wrong charge being made against Rogers. The Taoiseach, Charles Haughey, assured the House that a new charge was on the way: that of capital murder. It was clear though that Rogers was going to have to be released before being recharged.

Rogers underwent an operation to remove the bullets from his left foot. He remained in Wexford County Hospital for three days while the legal row continued inside and outside the Dáil.

Technically, Peter Rogers was not in custody from the withdrawal of the first charge until the preferring of the second charge, that of capital murder. But during that time his hospital bed was surrounded by armed gardaí.[1] Rogers' solicitor, Garret Sheehan, turned up at the hospital and tried to gain access to him. Gardaí searched the lawyer before allowing him into the ward. Two detectives remained in the room and refused to leave when Sheehan requested privacy with his client.

In an unusual legal move that Saturday, the Special Criminal Court sat as both the Special Criminal Court and the High Court. It was the day on which the accused was being rearraigned on the capital murder charge. Detectives had to carry Rogers into the dock with a heavy bandage covering his leg wound. The armed guard, Superintendent John Galvin of Wexford explained to the court, was for Rogers' own protection.

'Arrangements were made to protect Rogers from any person who might be likely to make an attack on him,' Galvin said.

'Including his own solicitor?' responded counsel for the defence, Patrick MacEntee.

'I gave instructions that people were to be taken charge of … gardaí were to make quite sure no unauthorised person was to see Rogers. This was because there was always the possibility that someone might come in with a gun or a knife, and try to kill him.'

---

1   The complex sequence in relation to the arrest and charging of Rogers is as follows. He was first charged on Tuesday, 14 October, and this charge was withdrawn on 15 October. He was rearrested on 17 October and recharged on Saturday, 18 October, at the Special Criminal Court, having been free for one hour.

'Are you suggesting his solicitor, or even his own wife, was liable to assassinate him?' MacEntee asked, eyebrows rising.

'I would not say she would be likely to assassinate him, but there could be a question of bringing in deleterious materials, poisons, or something like that.'

Galvin denied that Rogers had been in custody in the period between the withdrawal of the first charge and the preferring of the second: he was free to leave at any time.

'And when he did was immediately rearrested and was at all times surrounded by armed members of the Garda Síochána and was accompanied down hospital steps by a man with a machine-gun?'

'I can't agree,' said Galvin.

Rogers had discharged himself from hospital on the Friday night. A garda on duty at the hospital relayed the news to Galvin, who rushed to the hospital and was there with seven other gardaí when Rogers came out.

'Was it your intention to arrest him immediately after he left the hospital?' Mr Justice Liam Hamilton, presiding, enquired.

'Yes.'

Mr Justice Hamilton accepted a defence submission that Rogers was not in lawful custody. Rogers left the courtroom and went with friends and relatives to a nearby pub. He downed one glass of brandy and then drove off with his solicitor. One hour later he was arrested at the solicitor's home on foot of newly issued warrants from the Special Criminal Court for capital murder. He was now back in lawful custody.

A DAY earlier, gardaí from the Wexford division had formed a guard of honour at their slain colleague's funeral. They carried the coffin, draped with the tricolour and the dead detective's cap on top, from the hospital chapel to the waiting hearse. Most of the population of the town turned out to line the route as the mile-long cortège wound its ways through the narrow streets from Wexford County Hospital to the church on Bride Street. Among the hundreds of mourners was Detective Donal Lyttleton, who cried openly as his friend and colleague was buried. Members of the 1960 hurling team who had celebrated with James Quaid the day they won the all-Ireland medal also joined in the cortège. It was one of the biggest funerals Wexford had ever seen. The Bishop of Ferns, Dr Donal Herlihy, said the killing brought home to all 'how dangerously the forces of law and order have to live in these times'. The whole country had just witnessed a further escalation of the violence that had become almost endemic in recent years. Wexford in particular, he said, had watched one of its own being gunned down, his life snuffed out in the discharge of his duty.

During the previous few days, a row had blown up over the refusal by the GAA to call off its matches as a mark of respect to Detective Quaid. The former Kerry footballer Mick O'Connell accused the organisation of 'shirking its responsibilities' towards its former members. James Quaid was the third garda to have been murdered that year: the previous July, John Morley and Henry Byrne had been gunned down. The GAA had not cancelled its matches after their murders either. Calling them off would not bring the dead garda back, O'Connell said, but it would be a clear indication of the GAA's concern about the political violence spilling into the Republic. The organisation had, in the past, been accused of paying only lip-service on the national question. Now, he would accuse the GAA of ambiguity.

After he had been charged with capital murder, Peter Rogers

was taken to the high-security prison at Portlaoise, where he immediately went onto the Provo landing. His trial opened in the Special Criminal Court in February 1981, four months after the killing of James Quaid. He pleaded not guilty. The trial lasted for fifteen days, and on 11 March, Peter Rogers was convicted of capital murder and possession of firearms and explosives. Delivering the verdict, the presiding judge, Mr Justice Thomas Doyle, said that when Rogers went for his gun on that fateful night it was loaded and ready for immediate use:

> He proceeded to use it. After the first shot, followed by the departure of Lyttleton, he concentrated his attention on Quaid. When Quaid's first shot passed close to him, he could have made clear he was surrendering and thrown down his gun. Instead, he fired four separate shots at Quaid's position as indicated by the gun flashes. In the opinion of the court, it is inescapable that his intent was to incapacitate Quaid by killing or seriously injuring him. He succeeded in carrying this into effect.

After delivering the verdict, the judge asked Rogers if he had anything to say. 'No,' he replied in a voice that was barely audible in the packed and hushed courtroom. Mr Justice Doyle then went on to pronounce the death sentence: 'The court orders and directs that you, Peter Rogers, be now removed from this courthouse to the prison in which you were last confined and that you be there detained in custody and that on 6 April 1981, you there suffer death by hanging.'

The only sound that could be heard in the courtroom as sentence was passed was the bitter sobbing of Rogers' wife, Deirdre. Three of the condemned man's sisters and other relatives were there beside her in the public gallery. Peter Rogers was the fourth man in as many months to have been condemned to death for the killing of a garda. Peter Pringle, Colm O'Shea and Patrick McCann were already under sentence of death for the murder of Garda Henry Byrne.

Peter Rogers' death sentence was subsequently commuted to forty years' imprisonment without remission. In the following years, Deirdre Rogers campaigned for her husband's release. While in Portlaoise, Rogers fell out with the Provos. He felt that the organisation was not doing enough for the 'forty-year men'. He left the IRA landing and moved down to the prison 'bunker', where non-aligned prisoners such as the maverick republican Dessie O'Hare were confined.

On 22 December 1998, Peter Rogers became a free man again when he was released under the Good Friday Agreement. He had gone to prison as a Provo and as such was covered under the terms of the agreement. He never returned to Wexford. He and his wife and son moved to Dundalk, where he has since attempted to start his own business. He is still living there.

7

Garda Patrick Gerard Reynolds

৵৵ৎৎ

S hortly after ten o'clock on the morning of Friday, 16 May 1997, a car pulled up outside the Bank of Ireland at Main Street in Foxford, a small County Mayo village lying midway between Castlebar and Ballina. It had been stolen in Northern Ireland and fitted with false Dublin number plates. The driver parked the car, walked into the bank and pulled out a sawn-off shotgun. Garda Noel Canavan was off duty that morning and was walking past the bank when, for some reason, he noticed the tall, slim man going in. Once inside the bank the raider held the shotgun in his right hand and stood just inside the door, where he had a clear view of the bank floor. He held a bag in his left hand and levelled the gun at two officials behind the counter. He threw the bag at them. 'Fill that,' he ordered, in a distinct Northern accent, while pointing the gun at their heads. He let off one shot to show that he meant business. Outside on Main Street Garda Canavan heard the shot and rang the gardaí in Swinford. Inside, the bank officials were scooping bundles of cash into the bag at gunpoint.

Clutching the bag of cash, the raider ran out, made his way to the car and was slinging the shotgun onto the front seat when Canavan made a grab for him. A passer-by saw the struggle and ran to help the off-duty garda. The raider tried to reach the shotgun on the seat of the car but the passer-by got there first. Grabbing the gun, he emptied two cartridges from it, one live and one spent. A local publican, spotting the mêlée, ran to the car, got the raider in a headlock and held him until the gardaí arrived from Swinford, minutes later.

Gardaí bundled him into the patrol car and took him to Swinford Garda Station. They found £3,090 cash in the bag, the proceeds of the bank raid. The Northern Ireland man had a skull and crossbones tattooed on his arm, underneath the words 'Death Before Dishonour'. On his left arm 'IRA' had been blotted out and covered by the word 'Rose'. At some stage, he had had another tattoo — 'BAP' — symbolising the firearm Browning Automatic Pistol. Alarm bells were now beginning to ring. One of the gardaí put a call through to the Crime and Security Branch in garda headquarters, suggesting that they send a couple of Special Branch detectives down to Swinford. The senior officers were to confirm what the local gardaí had suspected: their bank raider was none other than Seán 'Bap' Hughes, the Belfast INLA man who was chief suspect for the murder of Garda Patrick Reynolds in Dublin in 1982. He had been on the run for fifteen years. His luck had just run out.

IN FEBRUARY 1982, Garda Patrick Reynolds was stationed at Tallaght, a sprawling suburb of County Dublin heavily populated with young couples and families. It was a million miles away from Reynolds' home in Barroe, County Sligo, a small townland of rolling hills and white stone walls overlooking Lough Arrow, a few miles from the Roscommon border. In 1982, Tallaght Garda Station was located in a small, single-storey building on the edge of the village, beside an old stone church. Reynolds had joined the gardaí in 1978 and had come to Tallaght as a young recruit. He and three other gardaí shared a house in the village.

Reynolds was on duty in the early hours of Saturday, 20 February. It was a normal Friday night/Saturday morning, with gardaí dealing with the usual after-hours problems but nothing out of the ordinary. At 1.30 a.m. an anonymous phonecall came through to the station. Garda Patrick Lally picked it up. A number of people were acting suspiciously at a flat in Avonbeg Gardens, the caller said. Three men had been seen carrying black bags into the flats. Lally told Sergeant Patrick O'Brien about the tip-off. The sergeant called four other gardaí — Reynolds, Leo Kenny, Larry McMahon and Tom Quinn — and said they had better get over to Avonbeg and check it out.

Avonbeg, a local authority flats complex at the far end of the village, was made up of three-storey buildings with dark, winding stone staircases and fire escapes at the rear. The local authority had installed halogen lights on the ceilings of the landings to light the stairwells at night. It was a run-down complex and a well-known haunt for squatters and transient drug users. It was not unusual to see discarded syringes, beer cans and bottles strewn around the open space in front of and behind the flats. Number 33 was on the first-floor landing.

Two days before the anonymous tip-off, the Bank of Ireland in Askeaton, County Limerick, had been robbed. It had just opened for business on Thursday morning when a gang of armed and masked raiders vaulted the counter and threatened to blow the heads off the staff. One of the gunmen had forced the bank manager, Thomas Kelly, to open the strongroom while an accomplice forced the staff in at gunpoint. They made off with £62,100 in cash. It was a well-planned job. The cash had been delivered just thirty minutes before the gang struck. All members of the gang escaped safely with the cash.

It was just after 1.30 on Saturday morning when the squad car pulled up outside Avonbeg. Reynolds and O'Brien went around the back of the flats. Kenny, McMahon and Quinn went up to the first-floor landing. All five gardaí were unarmed. Leo Kenny forced open the door of number 33 and startled a man and two women who were inside. He heard movement coming from the bathroom, where the door was slightly ajar. There were three men inside, counting wads of cash. A sub-machine-gun, a Ruger rifle and a semi-automatic pistol lay beside them on the floor.

The gardaí drew their batons as the gang tried to reach to the floor for their guns. One of them aimed at Kenny and squeezed the trigger but it misfired. The next shot lodged in Tom Quinn's baton, almost splitting it in two. The gardaí backed off. Patrick O'Brien, who was still at the back of the building, saw a man trying to escape through a small window. Underneath the window was a set of railings and, on the other side, open green fields. The man looked as though he was about to jump, but spotted Garda Reynolds and Sergeant O'Brien below, and ducked back inside. The sergeant asked Reynolds to go around to the front of the building while he remained at the back, in case anyone tried to escape from the rear. Reynolds heard the shots and ran around towards the front stairwell to see what was happening. Just then Larry McMahon came running out to O'Brien. 'There's a lot of guns round there,' McMahon said. Reynolds was running up the stone stairs and had just reached the top when he came face to face with one of the gunmen. Garda Reynolds turned to back away from him just as the gunman fired two shots from a .38 revolver, hitting Reynolds once in the back. O'Brien was looking up and saw the two flashes and the gunman illuminated by the halogen light over his head. With a bullet in his back, Reynolds continued to come down the steps. Stumbling, he collapsed unconscious in the hallway.

O'Brien was now standing at the entrance to the hallway. Over his shoulder he saw two men running from the front of the building towards a red Ford Escort car, one of them carrying a gun. The gunman jumped into the driver's seat, the second man got into the passenger seat and they took off at high speed. Garda Reynolds was lying where he had fallen. Having entered through his back, the .38 bullet travelled down, ricocheted off his ribs and pierced the valves of his heart. He bled to death on the ground. He was twenty-three years old.

PATRICK REYNOLDS came from a farming background and was third eldest in a family of five boys and one girl. He was known to his family and friends as Gerard, never Patrick. Journalist Marese McDonagh had been an old school friend of Garda Reynolds. At the time of the murder she wrote in the *Kerryman* newspaper about the man she knew as a boy:

> The papers were a bit confused about whether he was Pat or Gerry and whether he was 24 or 26. Actually he was 23 and he was known as Gerard to all of us around Barroe, the townland in County Sligo where he grew up. He went to Cloonagh school on the shores of Lough Arrow which meant he was one of a troupe of families who came 'down

the rock' to school, which if you don't know the geography of the area and don't know about all the hills and white stone walls, won't make much sense to you. Gerard was nice, a bit of crack ... he was the last person you'd think of when the news bulletin mentioned Garda Reynolds' murder. I did see him once in Dublin on his patrol bike, but as usual he was joking. He flashed the lights at two of us who were up from the country and then, when he stopped to be sociable, his bike wouldn't start again.

Frank Reynolds was due to join the gardaí on the Wednesday after his brother's death. He put it off for a year, but subsequently joined up and is now stationed at Granard, County Longford. He had made arrangements to meet up with Patrick that Saturday for a rugby match:

On the Friday evening my sister, Mary, her husband, John, and myself travelled to Dublin for the international rugby match at Lansdowne Road on Saturday. Mary spoke to Gerard by phone from Maynooth. She arranged with him that we would all meet on Saturday. Early on Saturday morning the gardaí from Fitzgibbon Street called to the house where I was staying. They told me that Gerard had been involved in an accident. They accompanied me to the Meath Hospital, where they had taken Gerard. My parents were told the news by the gardaí in Boyle. They were both in a state of shock. It was devastating.

Patrick's mother, Molly, died in 1987, his father, Paddy, in 1999. 'They never got over it,' said Frank:

To this day, it's hard to put it into words. I suppose grief is very private and personal to oneself. Gerard's death is not something we can easily talk about. Everyone was very good at the time, people who came [to sympathise] and remained friends of the family. Our neighbours of course were, and still are, wonderful. But no matter how good people are, it's your loss and you have to cope with it and it's very hard. In every family, but particularly a farming family, there is a unity, and each person has their place and role in the home and farm. That unity was broken by Gerard's death.

Garda Reynolds' remains were brought to Mount Argus Church in Dublin, where a sea of blue uniforms filled the pews as his coffin was carried up the aisle. Among the hundreds of wreaths were dozens from the people of Tallaght, where the young garda had been a familiar figure on his patrol bike. His body was then brought home to the west of Ireland for burial in the rocky County Sligo countryside. Two local traditional musicians, a fiddler and a flautist, played at his funeral Mass in Highwood, the church in which he had been baptised. 'After we got over the shock of Pat's death we felt that his funeral should embody the love local people had for him,' said Sligo curate Fr Noel Connolly. 'He was just an ordinary lad who always looked forward to his weekends off so he could return home.' After the Mass, six garda outriders escorted the tricolour-draped coffin on the slow journey along five miles of winding road to Ballyrush Cemetery. 'We have never seen the likes of it before and I hope we never will again,' said a garda on point duty.

THE MURDER of Patrick Reynolds caused widespread public revulsion. The brutal manner of his death, as much as his youth, sickened people. An opinion poll carried out on the day he was buried showed that a majority of people (64 per cent) were in favour of executing those convicted of capital murder. Around the time of the murder, the Fine Gael/Labour coalition government (which was shortly to lose office) proposed to introduce a bill abolishing the death penalty. This was despite strong opposition from its conservative element, particularly Patrick Cooney, a former Minister for Justice. In the aftermath of the Reynolds killing, Fianna Fáil indicated it would not support the bill. Coming so soon after the killing, the opinion poll reflected public outrage in the high percentage in favour of execution. It is doubtful if the figure would have been as high if the poll had been carried out in a calmer climate when feelings were not so inflamed.

At that stage, the murder investigation, based at Crumlin Garda Station, was well under way. Straight after the killing, gardaí set up roadblocks on all major roads in and out of the capital. The first arrests occurred almost immediately. Two men and a woman detained near the scene were taken to Tallaght Garda Station for questioning. The woman, who was from Firhouse in Templeogue, County Dublin, was a girlfriend of one of the men who had been in the Avonbeg flat. The three were subsequently released without charge, although one man was later charged with the Askeaton robbery. Gardaí had recovered from the flat a holdall full of cash — the proceeds of Askeaton — two semi-automatics, an armalite rifle, a Lugger pistol and two magazines for one of the firearms. They also found a pair of small round-framed glasses and a fingerprint.

The finger of blame was quickly pointed at the INLA. The gardaí released a description of two men they wanted to question. One was about twenty-eight years old, with dark brown hair, of medium build and five feet eight inches in height. The other was described as twenty-five years old, five feet eleven inches tall, with dark hair. On 26 February, the INLA issued a statement denying responsibility for the murder of Garda Reynolds, claiming he had been shot dead by 'rejects' of the organisation:

> The Irish National Liberation Army disclaims all responsibility for the shooting of Garda Reynolds in Tallaght, Co. Dublin or the recent bank robbery at Askeaton, Co. Limerick. The Irish National Liberation Army … has never been involved in the shooting of either gardaí or civilians in the 26 counties. We will no longer tolerate or accept responsibility for the actions of rejects from our organisation.

The trouble was, nobody believed them. Seán 'Bap' Hughes, a twenty-five-year-old INLA man from Albert Terrace on Belfast's Lower Falls, was top of the garda wanted list. Garda headquarters issued all garda stations with a detailed description and told them to be on the lookout for him. Gardaí also alerted all air and sea ports and issued overseas police forces with a photofit of the man they wanted to question. Later that year, the gardaí caught up with Hughes in Paris. He had been under surveillance by French police and British intelligence. They also had an interest in him. The French authorities set up an informal identification procedure. (The way in which informal identification procedures normally operate is that police officers are brought to the vicinity in which the suspect is known to either live or frequent; it is then up to the individual police officers to make a positive identification.) Sergeant Patrick O'Brien, Garda Tom Quinn and a senior detective, Edward Ryan, travelled to France in late October to see could they identify Hughes as the man on the stairwell in Avonbeg on the night of the murder. They did not recognise anyone on that occasion and returned to Dublin.

The following week Ryan told O'Brien and Quinn that they had to make a return trip to Paris. On the morning of 6 November, the three men were walking from their hotel to Gare St-Lazare when O'Brien was told to keep watch in the railway station concourse and in the adjoining Rue Amsterdam. O'Brien recognised a man coming towards him at St-Lazare and told French police he was satisfied that it was Seán 'Bap' Hughes. He said that he was the man he saw on the night of the Reynolds murder. Extradition proceedings were set in train in 1984 and rumbled on for three years. Ultimately, in 1987 the French courts refused the application. At that stage, Hughes was a prisoner in a French jail: the courts had sentenced him to four years for possession of a false passport. He served his sentence, grew a goatee beard and slipped back into Ireland sometime during the mid-nineties. The next time gardaí would see Hughes was in the quiet country town of Swinford, after the Foxford bank raid.

HUGHES WAS taken from Swinford Garda Station to Castlebar District Court, where he was charged with robbing £3,090 from the Foxford branch of Bank of Ireland on 16 May 1997 and with possession of a sawn-off shotgun on the same date. Hughes pleaded guilty, and in December 1997, the Special Criminal

Court jailed him for eight years. In June 1998, when Hughes was six months into his sentence at Portlaoise, Detective Inspector Martin McLaughlin travelled to the prison, where he served Hughes with new warrants issued by the Special Criminal Court. Hughes was now charged with the capital murder of Garda Patrick Reynolds on 20 February 1982 and with possession of an armalite rifle, a Ruger mini-rifle, an Uzi sub-machine-gun and a .38 semi-automatic pistol on the same date. He was also charged with the robbery of £62,100 at Askeaton on 18 February. His trial was set for April 1999 at the Special Criminal Court.

Almost as soon as it had opened the state's case ran into trouble over one crucial issue — identification. The prosecution case rested almost entirely on visual identification. Eamonn Leahy, prosecuting, told the court that Tom Quinn, who had since retired from the force, had changed his proposed evidence. Quinn had told the authorities days before the trial was due to begin that his visual identification of Hughes on the streets of Paris in 1982 was incorrect. Leahy then applied for an adjournment, which was opposed by Hughes' counsel, Paul McDermott. The identification happened seventeen years before and there appeared to be no supporting documents in France, he said. Further enquiries would reveal nothing more.

The state won an adjournment and the trial got under way the following March, by which time Quinn was prepared to identify Hughes as the man at the scene of the Reynolds killing. Patrick O'Brien, who had also since retired from the gardaí, was first into the witness box. 'I have no doubt that the man sitting in the dock today is the man I saw on the landing outside 33 Avonbeg Gardens,' he said. 'The accused, like all of us, has changed, he's wearing glasses now, but I have no doubt whatsoever that that is the man with the beard and the glasses.'

O'Brien told the court that after entering the building, he saw his colleague Garda Reynolds stumble and fall to the ground and he saw a gunman standing on the landing in the block of flats. 'I saw Garda Reynolds turn to come down the steps and I saw two flashes … I heard two shots being discharged. He was in the act of turning to come back down the stairs when I saw the flashes and heard the gun. It was a matter of seconds.'

O'Brien said that he had seen the gunman running out of the flats into a nearby car and take off at high speed. 'To this day I often think how did the other bullet miss me. I am convinced it went over my head.' The retired garda said that there had been sufficient light from the light in the ceiling of the flats to enable him to get a good view of the gunman. 'I was looking directly at them, my Lords, and I recognised the man who got into the driver's car. I got a full facial view of him, straight on.' Asked by McDermott if he had been aware of the involvement of the intelligence section of the British Embassy in Paris in the identification procedure in 1982, O'Brien replied 'No.'

A defence application seeking discovery of certain garda documents from 1983 to 1988, relating to Hughes' identification and his attempted extradition, was refused on the usual security grounds. Detective Chief Superintendent Dermot Jennings was the custodian of the files in his role as chief of intelligence of the Garda Síochána. Jennings appeared in court, briefcase in hand, but he was not prepared to hand over any of the crucial documents. Disclosure 'would have consequences for the security of this state and the security of other states,' he said. Claiming privilege, Jennings said that disclosure would expose a source of information and place that person in 'severe danger'.

The state's case fell on identification. On 6 April 2000, Hughes was acquitted of the capital murder of Garda Patrick

Garda Richard Fallon and his wife Deirdre. (Courtesy of the Fallon family)

Garda Inspector Samuel Donegan and his wife Mary. (Courtesy of the Donegan family)

Garda Michael Reynolds.
(Courtesy of Garda
Archives)

Garda Michael Clerkin.
(Courtesy of Garda Press
Office)

Detective Garda John Morley. (Courtesy of the Morley family)

Garda Henry Byrne. (Courtesy of Garda Archives)

Detective Garda James Quaid. (Courtesy of Garda Archives)

Garda Patrick Gerard Reynolds. (Courtesy of the Reynolds family)

Garda Sergeant Patrick McLaughlin. (Courtesy of the McLaughlin family)

Recruit-Garda Gary Sheehan. (Courtesy of the Sheehan family)

Detective Garda Frank Hand.
(Courtesy of Garda Press Office)

Garda Sergeant Patrick Morrissey.
(Courtesy of Garda Press Office)

Garda Sergeant Andrew Callanan.
(Courtesy of Garda Press Office)

Detective Garda Jerry McCabe.
(Courtesy of the McCabe family)

The car in which Jerry McCabe
was shot dead. The wires show the
trajectory of the bullets.

An AK47 bullet
fired in the fatal
blast, lodged in the
door panel.

Reynolds. He was also cleared of unlawful possession of firearms. The court accepted that Patrick O'Brien and Tom Quinn were 'manifestly truthful', but there was little corroboration, which was vital for a conviction. The fingerprint found in the flat was that of Hughes, but its presence was not proof of his involvement in the murder. It went no further than establishing that he had been in the flat a day or two before the incident, the court said. Similarly, while accepting 'beyond reasonable doubt' that the spectacles recovered at the flat belonged to the accused, they did not establish his presence at the time of the shooting. It was possible, said the presiding judge, Mr Justice Frederick Morris, that they could have been brought to the flat in his absence. There was nothing left but the uncorroborated evidence of dock identification.

Hughes' friends and relatives in the public gallery burst into applause and began cheering as the verdict was delivered. The dead garda's four brothers and one sister sat at the other side of the gallery, stunned.

Patrick O'Brien remains very disappointed at the verdict:

Pat was a grand lad; he came to me as a recruit from Templemore. He was one of twenty or thirty young fellows sent to Tallaght to build up the strength of the force there. It was desperate what happened to him. After the court case, letters came to me from all over the country from people who were disgusted at the outcome. They couldn't understand it. I felt we were made out to be liars. On the second visit to Paris, the time I saw him in Amsterdam Street, my heart leapt in my mouth. You know, when I was in the guards, I always regarded that when you brought someone to the steps of the court, well, your job was done and the courts take over. But this has made me very bitter the way it has turned out.

Seán 'Bap' Hughes served barely three years for the armed robbery at Foxford. He qualified for early release under the Good Friday Agreement and was freed on 22 May 2000. He has since returned to his native Belfast.

8

Garda Sergeant Patrick McLaughlin

Sergeant Patrick McLaughlin and his wife, Dolores, were asleep in their bedroom in the married quarters at Dunboyne Garda Station, County Meath. It was the early hours of Saturday morning, 9 April 1983, between twilight and dawn. Their four children were also asleep. The married quarters, a small, whitewashed building with a long driveway, is located a few yards from the garda station, within the same grounds. Patrick McLaughlin had been there six years, having been transferred on promotion from nearby Omeath, County Louth. At Dunboyne Garda Station, Sergeant McLaughlin was 'skipper'.

He shared a roster with Garda Pat Tierney, who lived next door. On the night of 8–9 April, Pat McLaughlin was off duty and enjoying the rest. He was a quiet, family man, with a serious, honest face and a ready smile. He was well known around the town of Dunboyne; he was also approachable: anyone in a spot of trouble knew they could call on Pat McLaughlin, at any hour of the day or night.

That night there had been a twenty-first birthday party in nearby Dunshaughlin. Among the revellers were two friends, Joseph Greene, an Air Corps private aged twenty-two, and Thomas McCool, a twenty-four-year-old motor mechanic. Sergeant McLaughlin had helped Greene get enrolled in the Air Corps to train as an aircraft technician by signing a reference recommending him for acceptance.

McCool had been on a drinking spree from earlier that day. He was nursing a grudge against Pat McLaughlin. A couple of months earlier, the young mechanic had slashed the tyres of a local publican's car and McLaughlin had caught him. McLaughlin was tough but fair: he was always willing to give first-time offenders a break. Instead of prosecuting McCool, the garda sergeant arranged for him to pay £200 compensation to the victim.

Joseph Greene had also found himself in a spot of bother with the gardaí. Sergeant McLaughlin and a member of the drugs squad had caught him with a small amount of cannabis; a prosecution for possession was pending. On the day of the party, Greene had gone drinking, firstly to the Mill House bar in Clonee where he downed seven pints of beer, and then to an off-licence where he bought two bottles of wine. He went to Dublin and drank them under a tree in the Phoenix Park. Greene was worried about the pending prosecution for possession of cannabis and the effect it may have on his career in the Air Corps. He went home and took four Valium tablets. He then met up with McCool; they bought a carry-out of six cans of lager and went to the party.

Sometime after 3 a.m., when the party was in full swing, Pat McLaughlin's name came up. McCool and Greene decided it was time to settle old scores. Someone mentioned a gun. Greene and

McCool went into the hallway and talked about 'sorting out McLaughlin'. The two went to Greene's home at Castlefarm Estate in Dunboyne and took from a press a double-barrelled shotgun belonging to Greene's father. In another press they found two cartridges. Greene loaded the gun. McCool drove Greene's Honda motorcycle the short distance to Dunboyne Garda Station. It was 4.20 a.m. Everything was in darkness and there was complete silence except for the running of the engine. Greene dismounted, went to the canopy-covered door and rang the bell. There was no answer. He kept ringing it persistently and suddenly a figure appeared at the bedroom window.

'Who's there?' Sergeant McLaughlin called out. 'I'm up here. What's wrong.'

'There's somebody there,' McCool whispered to Greene. 'There's the sergeant.'

Greene had the shotgun on his hip. He stood back a bit from the door, looked up briefly and pulled the trigger. The sound of breaking glass shattered the stillness of the night. Greene jumped back on the bike and threw the spent cartridge into the ditch as they drove away at high speed in the direction of the Navan road.

Pat McLaughlin fell backwards into the bedroom, slumping almost into a sitting position. The side of his head had been blown apart. One of his eyes was severely damaged: blood was everywhere. 'Pat! Pat!' Dolores McLaughlin screamed. There was no answer. Dolores put her hands on the window-sill and for a few brief seconds caught a glimpse of the speeding motorbike with something long across the pillion passenger's knees. It was the shotgun that had killed her husband, she later realised. She tried to lay her husband on his side from the sitting position. When she took her hands away and saw they were full of blood, she went hysterical.

The only telephone line was attached to the station next door. Niall, their teenage son, had been sleeping downstairs on a camp-bed. She shouted for him to run to the station and transfer the phone to the house. He ran past her up the stairs, saw his father with shoulder and head wounds and began to scream. The two girls, Ruth and Hilary, awakened by the commotion, came out of the back bedroom. Their mother tried to get them back in to shield them from the carnage in her own bedroom. Dolores McLaughlin shouted for Pat Tierney in the house next door. 'Pat has been shot,' she cried.

Patrick McLaughlin took the full force of the blast in the face, left shoulder and arm. Traces of powder burns found around the wounds indicated the close range at which he was shot. He received medical attention on the spot from a local GP, Dr McCabe, and was rushed to the Richmond Hospital in Dublin, where he was put on a life-support machine. He had suffered irreparable brain damage and was critically ill.

For three days he clung to life on the ventilator. Each day, one of his garda colleagues drove Dolores McLaughlin from Dunboyne to the Richmond. On 11 April, the doctors took the dying sergeant down for his last scan. Previous scans had shown extensive brain stem damage. The shot to the side of his face had lodged in the base of the skull and damaged the delicate brain tissue. The last scan showed that Pat McLaughlin was effectively brain dead. It was now a question of when, not if, the life-support machine would be turned off. He was forty-two years old.

NEARLY TWO decades later, the memories of the terrible events of the morning of 9 April 1983 are still fresh in Dolores McLaughlin's mind:

It's an awful thing to be killed, but when it's done in your own bedroom, and you're there, it's a terrible trauma. That night Niall had been working with horses and he was due to get up early the next morning, so he was sleeping downstairs on a put-me-up bed. I heard the doorbell ringing. I thought it was a row or something in the town; normally if there was something wrong they'd come to the house — it was a regular occurrence. I said to Pat, 'They might go away,' but they kept their finger on the bell, ringing and ringing. So he got up and pulled down the window. Then I heard a loud bang, just one bang, but so loud it was deafening. Pat must have seen it coming because he went to get back in. All you could see was blood, the whole side of his head was blown apart and his eye was in a terrible mess.

Having to tell her four children that their father was dead was the hardest thing she has ever had to do:

We were in the hospital and Dr Saiyad called me and said the scan did not go well and I may have to give permission to turn off the life-support machine. The doctor asked me 'Do you know what that means? It's an awfully hard decision to make.' I said 'Yes, I understand. I know he's going to die.' Pat's mother, Elizabeth, and my eldest son, Niall, were down in the hospital canteen and when they came back up I had given permission. It was terrible hard on his mother — Pat was an only son.

They stayed with Patrick McLaughlin until he died at 1.30 in the afternoon. Then they went home to Dunboyne, where the three youngest children were waiting on news of their father. Mark, the youngest, was only eight:

> Mark was on the couch and Dr McCabe was there. I said 'You're Daddy's dead' and put my arms around him. 'What does dead mean, Mammy?' he said. I said 'God must have needed your Daddy more than we did, so he took him.' 'I want my Dad and I don't like God,' he said.

Sergeant McLaughlin had applied for promotion to the rank of inspector a few months earlier. He had completed the exams and had done the interview just days before he was murdered. 'He was terrible easygoing, Pat. He loved his job,' his wife said. 'He was good with people, always looked at the person behind the summons, and had a great sense of humour. I never really had any reason to worry about him in his work. The only time I had cause to be worried was when he was stationed in Omeath and he was shot at by the IRA around Carlingford. I rang the station and they said he was okay.' During his period in Omeath, Pat McLaughlin was involved in the arrest of eight British SAS members who had made an incursion into County Louth in May 1976. He gave evidence at their subsequent trial in the Special Criminal Court in Dublin.

WHEN DOLORES met Pat McLaughlin he was 'a garda on a bike' from Mullingar. Pat's father was a train driver on the Mullingar to Sligo line. Pat had three sisters. Dolores' family owned a dance-hall and cinema in Prosperous, County Kildare. They began dating, mainly going to dances in Lawlor's in Naas. The couple married in 1966 and Pat was transferred to Trim, then to

Omeath on promotion and, lastly, to Dunboyne in 1977. They had a house in Avondale Drive in Trim, which they rented out while they were living in the married quarters in Dunboyne. They had decided to sell it just before Pat was murdered. He was a great family man, Dolores McLaughlin recalls with a smile.

> Pat loved the kids and his home life; didn't take a drink or smoke. He liked horses alright, but he couldn't afford to gamble much, not on a garda's wages. He liked golf and drama. He had a good singing voice, but when he sang a song at a garda function it was usually 'Three Wheels on my Wagon' because it was the only song that he could remember all the words of. He had great patience with the kids — an awful lot more than me. It was Pat who normally got up for them in the mornings. No good in the house though: he couldn't hammer a nail into a wall. I remember one time he tried to wallpaper. Well, that was a big mistake.

Patrick McLaughlin was buried at St Loman's Cemetery in Trim. The towns of Dunboyne and Trim came to a standstill. The hearse carrying the dead sergeant's remains from Richmond Hospital was accompanied into Dunboyne by a group of uniformed gardaí who had formed a guard of honour on the outskirts of the town. Behind the hearse came a Range Rover and trailer laden with wreaths from garda stations and depots throughout the country. There was also a wreath from the RUC. The parish priest of Dunboyne, Fr Edward Rispin, felt as though he had lost a very close relative: 'He was the loveliest type of man you could find. He was a man we all respected and loved. There's more than the ordinary feeling of loss — we feel a deep personal loss,' he said at the time of the murder.

In times of grief, small things take on a greater significance. Dolores McLaughlin does not forget the kindness extended to her and her children in the days and weeks following her husband's murder. But nearly two decades later, other, less considerate, events still rankle. One of these concerned local Fine Gael TD John Bruton, who was Minister for Industry and Energy at the time. His constituency includes Dunboyne. People were coming and going all the time in the days leading up to the funeral, Dolores McLaughlin recalls: 'Then a garda said "Someone wants to see you, he's just here." There was a state car parked at the end of the roadway — it didn't come up to the house.' Dolores walked down to the end of the driveway.

> There was a flick of a button and this hand came out. I heard a voice coming from the car saying 'I'm very sorry to hear about your husband.' It was John Bruton. He never so much as got out of the car to speak to me. The car stayed on the road outside the house. To this day I see that hand coming out the open window; I'll always see it. Michael Woods was the Opposition spokesman for Justice at the time and he was a gentleman. He called to the house and left me his number in case I needed anything; he was so nice and polite. Little things mean a lot at a time like that and I'll never forget his kindness.

SERGEANT PATRICK McLaughlin was the ninth garda to die since 1970 and the twenty-fifth since the foundation of the force. The garda associations were outraged, particularly since McLaughlin had been singled out for attack and shot in his own home. 'If we have come to the point of attacking gardaí in their own homes, in the presence of their families, then we have come to a sorry state of affairs,' Jack Marrinan, general secretary of the Garda Representative Association, said of the shooting. The Prison Officers' Association was more forthright. At the time of the McLaughlin murder, a prison officer, Brian Stack, was lying in a coma having been shot in the neck on a Dublin street. Republicans were suspected of having shot Stack in retaliation for what they claimed was his hard-line attitude towards republican prisoners. Prison officers were now calling for the extension of the death penalty to cover the attempted murder of members of the gardaí or the prison service.

A little over two hours after the shooting of Pat McLaughlin, the gardaí arrested Thomas McCool at Congress Park, Dunboyne. Five minutes later, at 6.40 a.m., they arrested Joseph Greene at his home at Castlefarm. Detective Garda Tim Mulvey of the investigation section of the Garda Technical Bureau and Detective Sergeant Gerry O'Carroll were present at Trim Garda Station when the two men were brought in. Greene appeared to be crying and was holding his head in his hands. 'I did it,' he admitted. 'I fired into the air. He was at the window; I heard glass breaking and got a fright. We only meant to break the window.' Greene agreed to make a written statement. In it he said that he had gone to the party in Dunshaughlin, where he and McCool decided to give McLaughlin a fright by firing a shot through his window. Greene had been in trouble over the cannabis and suspected that Sergeant McLaughlin had told his commanding officer in the Air Corps about it. 'I felt Sergeant McLaughlin was hounding me,' he said. 'I didn't mean to hit him. I remember saying to Tommy "I hope I didn't hit him."'

McCool's statement was similar in many respects. He and

Greene had talked at the party about sorting out McLaughlin, and then had gone to Greene's house to get the gun. The two stories dovetailed on the crucial aspect of intent — on which hinges the legal distinction between murder and manslaughter. In most murder trials the issue is not whether the accused killed the victim but whether, in killing, the accused *intended* to kill or cause serious injury to the victim. The crime of murder carries a mandatory life sentence, with a minimum of forty years for the capital murder of a garda. Manslaughter carries a discretionary penalty.

'We had decided that we would go up and give the sergeant a fright by discharging the gun,' McCool said. 'It was decided he should be got. We decided we would get Joe's shotgun and do the job tonight. Joe pointed the gun up to him and fired a single shot.' McCool said that he ran for the bike and started it up and Greene jumped on the back.

At 9.15 p.m. on 9 April, seventeen hours after the shooting, Greene and McCool were charged at a special sitting of the District Court with the attempted murder of Sergeant Patrick McLaughlin and possession of firearms with intent to endanger life. It was anticipated that a murder charge would follow, which it did a few days later, after Patrick McLaughlin died from his injuries. There were legal discussions over whether the charge should be one of capital or 'ordinary' — section 4 — murder (the section of the 1964 Criminal Justice Act which covers the murder of civilians). Because the sergeant was technically off duty, the charge fell under section 4. It was a decision that Dolores McLaughlin resents still.

McCool and Greene stood trial in the Central Criminal Court in Dublin in January 1985. They had pleaded not guilty to murder, even though they had made statements admitting to the killing of Sergeant McLaughlin. Patrick MacEntee prosecuted on behalf of the state. The trial — for the murder of a garda sergeant — lasted just four days, shorter than many trials for much less serious offences in the lower courts. Dolores McLaughlin was the chief witness for the prosecution. She cried as she relived the night of 8–9 April 1983. Until then, the family had lived a normal, happy life, she said. As she described the events that had shattered her life, her husband's killers sat a few feet away in the wooden-panelled courtroom.

Then it was Joseph Greene's turn to take the stand. He appeared in court dressed in the uniform of the Air Corps and was barely audible as he delivered his testimony to the jury. He did not deny carrying a loaded shotgun to Patrick McLaughlin's door, nor did he deny firing it at the garda sergeant. But, true to his statement of 9 April, he claimed that the intention had not been to kill or injure. He described getting off the bike at Dunboyne Garda Station and ringing the bell, but nothing seemed to be happening. 'Then I remember Tommy saying "There's somebody there."' He fired the single blast and heard the sound of breaking glass. 'I was very confused and I remember thinking I could not have hit anyone.' Greene threw away the spent cartridge into the ditch and remarked to McCool: 'I hope I did not hit him.'

A mitigating factor, Greene pleaded, was the cocktail of alcohol he had consumed on the night of 8–9 April. He said he had never drunk as much before and was worried that his pending prosecution for cannabis might have resulted in his being discharged from his job as an aircraft technician. Up until that point he had got on 'okay' with Sergeant McLaughlin. 'I am very sorry for what happened. I realise it was a stupid thing to do in the first place.'

Thomas McCool backed up Greene's testimony by swearing that they had only meant to frighten McLaughlin. 'I am deeply ashamed of myself for ruining this man's life, his career, the lives of his wife and family and my own family,' he told the jury.

Patrick MacEntee appealed to the jury of seven women and five men to bring in murder verdicts against both of them: it was a joint enterprise, and the prosecution did not accept that Greene was so drunk that he had been unable to form an intention. Thomas McCool's defence counsel, Seamus Sorohan, made an impassioned plea to the jury to accept the accused's sworn evidence that they had no intention to kill or injure the garda sergeant. Under law, he said, if one of the parties went beyond what was agreed upon in a joint venture, the second party, McCool, was not responsible for the first's unauthorised action. James Carroll, for Joseph Greene, asked the jury not to get 'carried away on a tide of indignation' but to accept Greene's evidence that there was no intention to kill or injure Sergeant McLaughlin.

The jury decided otherwise. Its members took four hours to bring in a verdict of murder against Joseph Greene. Thomas McCool was found not guilty of murder but guilty of manslaughter. Mr Justice Declan Costello imposed the mandatory life sentence on Greene and sentenced McCool to ten years' penal servitude. As the two men were being led away handcuffed, a friend of the late sergeant remarked: 'Justice has been done. Pat McLaughlin was tough but fair. He always gave the first-time offender a break.'

Greene and McCool were taken to Mountjoy Jail but were later transferred to the more relaxed Wheatfield Prison in Clondalkin, County Dublin, when it opened in 1988. Some time after, the *Gay Byrne Show* broadcast a radio programme from

Wheatfield. Joe Duffy was the reporter. That morning, Dolores McLaughlin listened to Joseph Greene being interviewed. It was the first time she had heard his voice since the trial:

> I was in the kitchen listening to the . . . programme and I heard him [Greene] on the radio. He was asked what was he in for and he said 'I killed a cop.' He had no remorse. If I had been warned about the programme, I might have listened to it and I might not, but at least I'd have been prepared for it. He said he had done a university degree in prison. What really annoyed me was that my eldest son was doing his degree at the same time and I had to pay for it and here was the man who had killed their father and the state paid for his. I still fume every time I think about it.

Niall, who was just sixteen when his father was murdered, is now a teacher. Hilary is also a teacher, Ruth a nurse. The youngest, Mark, works in the Irish Financial Services Centre in Dublin's docklands. Life has not been easy for Dolores McLaughlin, having to raise four children without their father. At times, the loneliness is crushing. After the murder, the family left the married quarters and moved back to Avondale Drive in Trim, to the house they had been planning to sell. Dolores still lives there.

> That was one of the worst times after Pat was killed. Moving on my own, driving after the lorry. We used to go off on Sundays on a drive with the kids. I remember one Sunday, shortly after we moved back. The kids were all heading off on their bikes and I remember thinking 'Jesus, is this me for the rest of my life?' Weddings were difficult;

my brother-in-law gave my daughters away. And graduations, they were hard because they should have been happy family times and Pat wasn't there to share them.

Thomas McCool was released from prison in 1992, Joseph Greene in September 1996. Between them they spent a total of eighteen years in jail for the killing of Patrick McLaughlin. They are now back in the workforce. Dolores McLaughlin thinks they got away lightly: 'It doesn't mean a great deal to me whether they're in or out, but they murdered someone and they should be made to serve more than a few years, especially Greene with his attitude. To think he has no remorse. He has his whole life to live and my children were left without a father. He got away Scot free as far as I'm concerned.'

In the intervening years, Hilary and Ruth, the young girls awakened from their sleep by the sound of the blast that killed their father, have had children of their own. Dolores McLaughlin plays with her two granddaughters and counts her blessings. As a family, they have remained very close. An expression of remorse from Thomas McCool or Joseph Greene to Dolores McLaughlin would have gone some way to easing the hurt, especially in the early years after the murder. It never came. The only personal expression of regret came from a relative of McCool:

Thomas McCool's aunt, a nun, wrote me a lovely letter saying she never thought a nephew of hers would do damage to anyone else. It doesn't change anything, but it helps when you know people are sorry. The other family never contacted me. Even if they had got in touch with me in some way, it would have meant something to me at the time. But it doesn't really matter now.

9

Recruit-Garda
Gary Sheehan and
Private Patrick Kelly

Our volunteers were involved in the abduction of Don Tidey and Friday's shoot-out at Ballinamore ... The abduction of Don Tidey and the ransom demand was related to the struggle in the North and the fatal shootings were clearly distinct from, say, a premeditated ambush on the Task Force[1] or Free State Army, which would be an attack on the institutions of the State.

IRA, 17 December 1983

T he republican movement was in freefall from 1976 onwards. By 1980, the IRA knew it could not force a British withdrawal from the North by purely military means. The armed struggle was going nowhere. Sinn Féin was, in political terms, very close to becoming a nonentity: it was weak, peripheral and largely ignored.

1 The Special Task Force was established in 1978 as a counter-strike force to subversive and serious crime. It was later subsumed into the Special Branch at Dublin Castle, later renamed the Special Detective Unit, now based at Harcourt Square, Dublin.

By the end of the 1981 hunger strike, during which ten republican prisoners died, the political landscape had changed utterly. The hunger strike had forced a major reappraisal within the republican movement. Although the electoral gains made during and immediately after the hunger strike were limited and, to some degree, transitory, the Provisionals realised that a political path to a united Ireland, rather than armed struggle, was the most viable option. The call by leading republican Danny Morrison at the 1981 Sinn Féin Ard Fheis for a twin-track policy of 'an armalite in one hand and a ballot paper in the other' heralded the emergence of a reorganised Sinn Féin and IRA. This was reflected in the replacement of the older, Southern leadership, who had little time for politics, by a younger, Northern leadership.

But this Northern surge of power and shift in policy was not without its problems. Internally, the republican movement was riven with dissent. The militarists wanted assurance that the move into electoral politics was not going to be at the expense of the armed struggle. Money was tight, and there was substantial resistance to diverting funds into fighting elections and away from the IRA. In 1983, the annual 'budget' of the Provisional IRA was around £1 million. At the time, its main sources of income were smuggling and bank robberies. The new strategy led the IRA to look for another, alternative source of cash: kidnapping.

Businessmen and bankers were the main targets. Top of the list were Ben Dunne, co-owner of Dunnes Stores, and Galen Weston, the Canadian millionaire who owned the Quinnsworth supermarket chain in the Republic. The IRA also kidnapped Shergar, a racehorse owned by the Aga Khan and valued at £10 million. The Provos reckoned that the operations would yield more than £2 million in ransom money — two years' annual running costs. The net gain was, in fact, a lot less. In political terms, the kidnapping spree was counter-productive and was to end in disaster in Ballinamore, a quiet country town in County Leitrim, in December 1983.

DON TIDEY may never have been kidnapped but for events that August in County Wicklow. Eight heavily armed members of the IRA were ambushed as they attempted to abduct Tidey's boss, Galen Weston, at his home in Roundwood. Weston's company, Associated British Foods, owned the Quinnsworth supermarket chain in the Republic. In the 1980s, Quinnsworth advertisements were regularly on television: its marketing manager, Maurice Pratt, was practically a household name. The IRA reckoned the Galen Weston organisation would pay a ransom sufficient to purchase the heat-seeking surface-to-air missiles it was anxious to acquire at the time.

Thirteen heavily armed detectives had hidden overnight in Weston's home, waiting for the IRA gang. They had had the IRA unit under heavy surveillance since Shergar's disappearance the previous February, but were also aware of the plan to kidnap Weston through an IRA informer. At 7.45 a.m., the gang burst into Galen Weston's courtyard. 'Gardaí. Drop your guns,' an armed detective shouted. The startled Provos were still reeling from the shock when the firing started. (The IRA later claimed that its members had been fired on without warning. The gardaí deny this.) Within seconds of opening fire, four IRA men fell to the ground, seriously wounded. One of them was the IRA's intelligence officer, Gerry Fitzgerald, who had been shot in the leg. The shooting continued, with the Special Branch firing

185 rounds of ammunition from sub-machine-guns. Three of the men escaped. In November, five of the would-be kidnappers were convicted of firearms offences and sentenced to up to fourteen years' imprisonment.

Roundwood was a disaster for the Provos, but they were not giving up. On 24 November 1983, as the Roundwood gang were just beginning their sentences, the IRA kidnapped Don Tidey, a forty-nine-year-old Englishman who had been living in Ireland for fifteen years. Don Tidey was chief executive of the Quinnsworth chain. He was a widower with a teenager daughter, Susan, and two adult sons, Andrew and Alistair, living in Woodtown Way, a quiet cul-de-sac in Rathfarnham, south Dublin. Tidey was also a man with regular habits, one of which was using the same route to drive Susan to school each morning.

It was 7.45 a.m. and not yet daylight when Don Tidey left his dormer bungalow. He was dropping Susan off at Alexandra College, in Milltown, before heading to work. The Provos were watching as he pulled away in his new, brown Daimler. He had gone only a short distance when he saw two cars, one with a flashing blue light, blocking the junction of Woodtown and Stocking Lane. The beige Ford Cortina had been stolen the night before from Thomas Downes, a parish clerk at Newcastle West, County Limerick. The yellow Ford Escort had also been stolen. Alistair Tidey, driving a russet red Fiat, was right behind his father. Don Tidey slowed down; then, sensing something was wrong, he tried desperately to put the car in reverse and accelerate back down the road. A man dressed as a garda was standing in front of the Cortina. He stepped forward and was now beside Don Tidey. He produced a sub-machine-gun and put it to Tidey's head. Two other men pulled Susan and Alistair from the cars and threw them by the roadside. Susan was screaming as she watched her father being driven off at high speed in the direction of the Dublin Mountains.

The kidnappers continued up Mount Venus Road, turned right and were heading towards Tallaght when they had a minor crash. They kept going at high speed towards Brigid Burke's public house in Tallaght. By the time Susan and Alistair Tidey raised the alarm, the kidnappers had changed cars and were making good their escape. Gardaí would later find the stolen cars in Maynooth. The Escort had been burned out.

'The minute we heard he'd been kidnapped we knew it was the Provos,' recalls a now retired senior security officer. 'We had a good idea who was involved. We knew the type of personnel they'd use and what they were capable of.' The Special Branch suspected that among the ringleaders were three of the thirty-eight republican escapees who had shot their way out of the North's Maze Prison in September. The Tidey plan was organised by an IRA unit in the south-west, the same unit that kidnapped Shergar. The Special Branch had information that a well-known Munster republican was one of the key people involved.

Within hours, the army was called in, and so began one of the biggest manhunts in the history of the state. To add to the security forces' problems, the INLA leader Dominic McGlinchey was also on the run at the time. 'Between the two, Tidey and McGlinchey, the country was being turned upside down.' The IRA was hoping to extort £5 million sterling from the Galen Weston organisation in return for Tidey — an astonishing sum given that he was merely the chief executive, not the owner, of the Quinnsworth chain. And with each passing day, the IRA's chances of getting the cash diminished.

On the day after the kidnapping, the hunt for the IRA gang switched to Tralee, in County Kerry. A couple, a man and a woman, were arrested and questioned about the abduction. They were released without charge. The gardaí began looking closely at anyone suspected of having republican links. Houses were raided; the usual suspects were rounded up. Not only were the gardaí no closer to finding Tidey or his captors, but they had no firm intelligence as to which part of the country they should be concentrating on.

FOUR DAYS after Tidey was taken hostage, gardaí switched their search from Kerry to Ballinamore, County Leitrim, but the next day, 29 November, they concentrated on the Maynooth and Celbridge area of County Kildare. They had found cars used in the kidnap there, but no sign of Tidey or the gang. The Fine Gael/Labour coalition government made it plain that it was totally opposed to the payment of a ransom. The day after the Minister for Justice, Michael Noonan, told the Dáil the government could not condone any money 'falling into the hands of paramilitary groups', Associated British Foods in London received a ransom demand of £5 million for the safe return of its chief executive. Meanwhile, the searches were continuing. On 5 December, two men and a woman were arrested in Navan in connection with the kidnap, but they were released without charge the following day.

It was now eleven days since Don Tidey had been kidnapped and the combined forces of the state — more than 4,000 gardaí, soldiers and Air Corps personnel — were no nearer to finding him. It was as though Tidey and his captors had disappeared into the ether. The raids continued, only now they were not confined to the homes of the usual suspects. During the second week of December, a priest returned to his Leitrim parish after spending a few days away. He found his housekeeper slightly agitated.

'Father, while you were away we were raided,' she said.

'Raided?' repeated the astonished cleric.

'Yes, Father, the guards were here and when they searched upstairs they even asked for the keys to the press you had locked before leaving.'

The searches yielded little. They then switched to an area north of Ballinamore, Derrada Wood. Ballinamore, with a population of less than 800, has a strong republican tradition. Rumour has it that during the IRA split of December 1969, the new Provisional IRA command structure was formulated at a meeting that took place in a room above a pub in the town. At that meeting were almost all the figures who were later to emerge as the leadership of the Provisional IRA. In subsequent years, gardaí were to have several confrontations with armed IRA men in and around Ballinamore. It was to an area just outside Ballinamore that Shergar was brought after the IRA took him from Ballymany stud farm in Kildare in February 1983. Gardaí believe the racehorse is buried somewhere in the Ballinamore region.

Economically, south Leitrim was a poor area, with little state or foreign investment. Historically, it was badly hit by emigration. The isolated countryside north of Ballinamore through Cromlin, Aughnasheelan up to the Cuilcagh Mountains and Derrada is rough terrain and desperately poor. Derrada Wood is a small forest up a sloping field, three miles north-west of Ballinamore and roughly twelve miles south of the Northern Ireland border. In 1983, the pines were young, and twigs and small branches were just beginning to sprout. From three to four feet up the huge tangle of trees were almost choked with brambles and briars. The area surrounding it was covered with dense undergrowth, making movement difficult. Nobody knew the geography better than the Provos, who held many a training camp in the region.

It was here, deep in Derrada Wood, that Don Tidey was held almost continuously after being taken hostage, in a dugout five by fourteen feet and five feet high. Whoever constructed the lair stretched a length of protective polythene covering across a ridge in the sloping ground, onto the top of the dugout and up two feet along the nearest trees. The polythene, which was expertly covered by sticks, brambles and other foliage, gave some protection against the biting December wind. It was almost totally dark inside and resembled the natural habitat of a small animal when it is hibernating, according to a source who later saw the dugout. Inside were bare provisions: canned food and a few cans of beer. Bales of hay served as seating. The dugout was almost impossible to see from a distance of more than a few yards. As a hiding place it was perfect.

Officially, gardaí say it was good detective work, and not information supplied by an IRA informer, that led them to Derrada Wood. They also point to the fact that they had been monitoring, covertly and overtly, the movements of all known republicans and republican sympathisers in the area. But this author has learned that the RUC Special Branch in Belfast had also supplied information to the gardaí that Tidey was being held at Ballinamore. The RUC got the tip-off either directly from an IRA informer or through a communication interception, most likely a telephone tap.

Ironically, in the light of events that November–December, the number of gardaí assigned to Ballinamore had been halved in the period immediately before the Tidey kidnapping. Despite the level of republican support in the town and surrounding areas, there were just five gardaí left. And the town's patrol car had also been withdrawn. Now with the huge influx of personnel, there was more than enough gardaí to keep tabs on known republicans. One, a leading IRA operator, was seen at a dance in the town a few days before Don Tidey was found. It was his presence, and the sighting of another republican outsider, that convinced Chief Superintendent J.J. McNally that something was afoot. McNally was an experienced police officer who had spent years pursuing the Provos around the border counties. Mainly as a result of the information supplied by the RUC, garda headquarters gave the go-ahead for 'Operation Santa Claus', which was launched on Tuesday, 13 December. The gardaí appeared so confident of finding Tidey in the Ballinamore area that on the Thursday the Garda Commissioner, Larry Wren, flew down to Leitrim on a 'special visit'.

Operation Santa Claus was made up of ten search teams, each unit consisting of a garda inspector, two sergeants, a local garda, two gardaí experienced in border searches, up to seven armed detectives and nine or ten rookies — recruits from the Garda Training College at Templemore, County Tipperary. An army member was to accompany each recruit. The units were quaintly code-named Rudolph 1 to 10. The staked-out area, extending to five or six square miles, was to be subdivided among the Rudolph units. The strategy was that, where possible, the units would move across the terrain in a uniform line; the man at each end would have some form of radio equipment with which to communicate with Ballinamore Garda Station — 'Echo Base'. Between Thursday night and Friday morning, several hundred extra gardaí were drafted into Ballinamore, along with a few hundred soldiers. Everything was now in place. The units were to fine-comb the land, inch by inch.

IN TEMPLEMORE, the talk among the young trainees was of the goings-on at Ballinamore. The word was that a large number of garda recruits were to be detailed to the search for Don Tidey. Most were delighted to be getting a taste of 'real' garda work before they finished training; they were eager to get going. On 14 December, fifty recruits were told that they were going to Ballinamore the following day. One of them was Peter Gary Sheehan, a twenty-three-year-old single man from County Monaghan. He was the eldest son of a garda detective, Jim Sheehan from Carrickmacross, who was stationed in the town. Recruit-Garda Sheehan reported for duty at Ballinamore Garda Station and was assigned to Rudolph 5. Also assigned to Rudolph 5 was Army Private Patrick Kelly, from Moate, County Westmeath. He was thirty-six and a soldier with the 6th Infantry Battalion. Private Kelly had just completed his fourth tour of peace-keeping duty with the United Nations UNIFIL troops in Lebanon. Just eleven weeks earlier, his wife, Catriona, had given birth to the couple's fourth child, a son.

Recruit-Garda Sheehan was never called by his first name; it was always 'Gary'. He was a tall young man with a shock of curly hair and was very popular among the other recruits. In five weeks' time, he would be taking part in the passing-out parade at Templemore Training College. In the meantime he was looking forward to the chance to do some real policing.

ON FRIDAY, 16 December, at around 10 a.m., a Special Branch raiding party surrounded a public house in Ballinamore owned by John Joe McGirl, veteran republican and vice-president of Provisional Sinn Féin. McGirl was one of seven men on the Provisional IRA's first Army Council, formed in December 1969.

He had served a number of jail terms in the 1960s. On one occasion, ammunition was discovered in the hearse McGirl was driving at Drumsna, between Leitrim and Roscommon. McGirl was no stranger to garda raids, so when the Special Branch descended on the pub, he demanded to see the search warrant. The gardaí handed him a copy. Within the hour, he was lifted and driven through Killashandra and Cavan to Castleblayney Garda Station. In a synchronised series of lifts, three others were arrested in the Ballinamore area.

While the arrests were taking place, Rudolph 5 completed its first check of the search area and was now working its way through a second area, about one mile from Derrada Post Office. One of the few buildings in the area was a joinery workshop owned by Bernie Prior. He had a brother called Hugh Prior, a farmer from Drumdowna Lane. Joe McGirl, a nephew of John Joe's, used to do a few odd jobs at the joinery. Around the same time John Joe McGirl was being driven to Castleblayney Garda Station, gardaí spotted a young man running from a field within the Rudolph 5 search area. At lunchtime, Joe McGirl was arrested near the spot where the young man had been seen running from the field. He told gardaí he was on his way to town for a haircut.

While this was happening, Hugh Prior was driving from a friend's house back to his own home at Drumdowna in a blue Cortina. He had driven a short distance when he found his path blocked by a line of uniformed gardaí, armed detectives and soldiers. 'You are being arrested under section 30 of the Offences Against the State Act. Get out of the car,' a detective ordered. Prior was searched on the roadway and a uniformed garda got into the driving seat of Prior's car. Hugh Prior was ordered back into the car — into the front passenger seat — and an armed detective sat in the back. The garda then took off at high speed for Ballinamore Garda Station.

It was just after lunchtime, around 2 p.m., when members of Rudolph 5 began moving into Derrada Wood under the command of Detective Inspector Bill Somers. It was an extraordinary sight: soldiers in full combats with blacked-out faces carrying FN self-loading rifles mingling with Special Branch detectives, some wearing paramilitary-style protective clothing, all carrying Uzi sub-machine-guns, moving through a wood in quiet County Leitrim in the run-up to Christmas week. As they lumbered through the thicket, beating their way through the undergrowth, two gardaí and a soldier approaching from a western direction thought they spotted something. They were about to withdraw and call for reinforcements when Gary Sheehan, approaching from a different direction, came across a low earthen bank fifteen yards in front of him. A figure dressed in green army-style pants, a green combat jacket and knee-high black boots was crouching beside it. He was holding a white cloth in his hands and appeared to be cleaning a long-barrel rifle, similar to the army's FN standard issue.

Patrick Kelly was directly behind Recruit-Garda Sheehan as they approached the earthen mound. The young garda said something to the man with the rifle but got no answer; he was unsure whether he was a member of another search unit. A few feet away a garda sergeant, sensing something was wrong, called for assistance. Gary Sheehan turned around to Private Kelly. He was in the process of telling him that some army man in front would not answer him when a burst of automatic rifle fire rang through the forest, drowning out his last words. The young garda slumped to the ground, his face and the side of his head a mass of blood. 'Get back, get back, get out of the forest,' someone shouted.

There were more loud bangs as the armed members of Gary Sheehan's unit returned fire. The gun battle was brief but fierce. Another recruit-garda, Joseph O'Connor, heard a moan or grunt where Sheehan had been standing. Private Kelly had been hit by the gunfire and was now lying motionless on the ground beside a clump of young saplings. He had multiple body wounds. A few feet to the right lay the body of Gary Sheehan. Both men were dead.

A LOCAL pensioner, Peter Fee, was cycling to Derrada Post Office when he heard the shots ring out in the surrounding hills and noticed a lot of frenzied army activity. A few seconds after the shots a huge bang, like the sound of something exploding, could be heard for miles. In the few seconds the gun battle was raging, Recruit-Garda Joseph O'Connor spotted a bearded man dressed in combats lying on the ground facing towards him. He was signalling with his hands and whispering what sounded like 'Tidey — hostage'.

Within seconds of opening fire, the IRA kidnappers threw a stun grenade towards the searchers closest to them. It was the sound of the stun grenade Peter Fee and others had heard. While the security forces were reeling from its effects, the IRA men made their break for freedom. Grabbing their nearest adversaries — two gardaí and one soldier — and ordering them to run in front towards the top of the wood, the IRA men raced like hares through the scrub. They disarmed the hostages before releasing them just before they came to the top of the wood. The gang then emerged from the wood dressed in combats and managed to overpower two soldiers who were providing cover for the members of Rudolph 5 inside the wood. Still running, and with weapons seized from their garda hostages, they headed towards the open fields where they had a good view of the approach road to the hillside.

The Provos' good fortune was to hold out. They managed to commandeer a blue Opel car near the spot where they had escaped. The events of the next few minutes are mired in confusion and controversy and could well have had tragic consequences. Before the gun battle erupted, a garda car had been parked at the junction of the road leading to Derrada Wood. A garda assigned to the patrol car saw gunmen in the blue Opel that was now speeding up behind him. Moving quickly to block their exit, he manoeuvred the patrol car across the roadway. Gardaí and troops began exchanging fire with the gunmen in the Opel. 'The Provos are shooting from a blue Opel car,' came a voice over the garda radios.

Just at this moment Hugh Prior's blue Cortina came on the scene at the other side of the wood. The arresting gardaí, unaware of the drama in Derrada Wood, were taking Prior to the garda station via the road below Derrada. There was just one radio communication from Ballyconnell, which meant the same message — 'The Provos are shooting from a blue Opel car' — was still being transmitted over some garda radios. By now there was total confusion. Armed gardaí and troops at the Swanlinbar side of the wood shot at the blue car —Hugh Prior's — in rapid bursts of fire. There was a loud bang as one of the bullets came through the rear window of the Cortina, nicking Hugh Prior on the back of the neck.

'I'm shot, I'm shot,' Prior screamed.

'Don't fire — there are gardaí and a prisoner in this car,' shouted the armed detective from inside the Cortina.

The firing ceased. Hugh Prior's blue car, with gardaí in it, coming on the scene at the same time as the Provos were trying to escape in the blue Opel presented them with a golden opportunity. With the patrol car blocking the road, the gunmen abandoned the Opel and made a break for the northern hills, one of them spraying gunfire to keep the security forces at bay.

AFTER THE first gun battle, in which Sheehan and Kelly were killed, Tidey had made his own break for freedom. He ran through the undergrowth in the green-and-brown paramilitary clothing his captors had forced him to wear. As he emerged from the thicket, a garda and a soldier nabbed him. They did not believe this unshaven, haggard-looking man in combats was the kidnap victim, Don Tidey. They thought he was one of the kidnappers; he thought they were Provos. It is a matter of luck, given the intensity of the situation, that he was not shot.

There was some pushing and shoving. The gardaí forced Tidey to the ground with his hands over his head, stripped him of his shoes, then frogmarched him down the field two hundred yards towards the approach road to Derrada Wood. It was at this precise moment that the Provos' blue Opel came speeding up behind them, spraying a hail of bullets at the gardaí, who returned fire. Detective Inspector Bill Somers and Detective Garda Donal Kelleher, who by now realised Don Tidey's true identity, were standing beside him. Kelleher threw himself between Tidey and the gunmen and got shot in the legs.

The entire operation was a disaster for the security forces. Two men were lying dead in Derrada Wood; two others, a detective and a civilian, were wounded; and the kidnappers, although heavily outnumbered, had managed to escape. And now there was a delay in reinforcements arriving because transport vehicles were not immediately available. Several young recruits, Gary Sheehan's colleagues, were admitted to Cavan Hospital suffering from shock; some were led in crying with blankets over their shoulders.

It was almost two hours before reinforcements were ready to begin a proper search for the gunmen. By that time it was nearly dusk and the kidnappers had put enough distance between themselves and Derrada Wood to make good their escape. Don Tidey was brought to Ballyconnell Garda Station and then to Cavan, where shortly after 4 p.m. he was examined by a local GP, Dr McDwyer. He had cuts and bruises on his face and was badly shaken but otherwise unharmed. Don Tidey was put into an upstairs room at a house on Main Street. Chief Superintendent J.J. McNally spent some time talking to him, making sure he was okay. Just before 6 p.m., McNally left the room and came down to talk to the throng of reporters who had converged on Cavan to report on Don Tidey's rescue.

'How do you feel after the day's work?' asked one reporter.

'It was an excellent day's work, saddened unfortunately by the deaths of two very brave young men who set out to play their part and who played their part in trying to arrest those … desperadoes … is the only thing I can describe them as …'

By this stage, gardaí and reporters were trying to piece together exactly what had happened in Derrada Wood. Lieutenant-Colonel Pat Dixon, military commander of the search, denied suggestions that the security forces had fired first. 'The first shots were definitely not fired by us. Our men were shot down in cold blood,' he said.

Don Tidey rang home to tell his children that he was safe and sound. He did not immediately mention the deaths of Gary Sheehan and Patrick Kelly. Back in Dublin, shoppers at

Quinnsworth in Crumlin and Rathfarnham heard the news of Tidey's release over the stores' tannoy system. For a few seconds there was dead silence; then the customers burst into clapping and cheering. After twenty-three days as an IRA hostage, Maurice Pratt's boss was finally coming home.

THE NINE o'clock news on RTÉ led with the dramatic headline that Don Tidey had been safely rescued in a shoot-out and was on his way back to be reunited with his family. The second line was that a garda and a soldier had been killed in the crossfire. Frank McNally was watching the news at home in his flat in Ballsbridge. McNally is now an *Irish Times* journalist. In 1983 he was in the civil service, but like the rest of the country, he was following with interest events at Ballinamore: 'They didn't name them, but I remember the newsreader saying the army had surrounded the woods and were waiting until dawn to go in and recover the bodies. I still had no idea who they were, but I remember thinking of them lying there all night,' he told this author. 'You can't but be impressed by two ordinary guys giving their lives to save someone else's and reunite them with their family.'

Before the end of the news bulletin, McNally got a call from his sister. She asked him if he knew who had been killed. 'I got a bit of a drop because the way she said it, I knew it had to be someone I knew.' His sister told him that the dead garda was Gary Sheehan, an old school friend of McNally's. He and Sheehan had applied to join the Garda Síochána around the same time, but McNally had changed his mind at the last minute:

The last time I saw Gary was when we were waiting for the medical for the guards. I decided to stay on in the civil service and I never knew Gary had been called up until that moment when I heard he'd been killed. It was a complete shock. I remember someone saying something to me when I got the news and I couldn't answer. It was probably the only time in my life that I could not actually speak.

Gary Sheehan and Frank McNally attended the same schools — St Joseph's National School in Carrickmacross and then on to the Patrician Brothers.

As a class, none of us were academically brilliant but I suppose Gary was the nearest thing in the class to a golden boy. There was no system of class prefect but if we had, it would probably have been Gary. But he was equally liked by fellow students and teachers. I remember he was good at sports, GAA; he was quite lean. In 1978, our class won the county championship. We beat Castleblayney in the final. I remember he scored two goals in the finish; he was certainly one of the heroes of the team that day. He was always called Gary, never Peter, but his nickname was 'Scurry'; I've no idea where it came from. Towards the end of fourth or fifth year he managed to persuade people to stop using it. It was only after he was killed that we found out his last name was Mary; if we'd known that at the time, he'd have got an awful slagging.

In 1978/9, McNally and Sheehan studied for the repeat Leaving Certificate. As McNally put it, 'four or five of us underperformed to some degree'. Halfway through, Sheehan decided to leave school. He went to work in the Wrangler jeans factory in Galway and began sharing a house with a couple of other lads his own age in the Newcastle area. The last time he and his old school friends got together was in September 1979, the weekend Pope John Paul II came to Ireland. McNally recalls:

> About a dozen of us, all old school pals, stayed the weekend in Gary's. We were young, Catholic and the Pope was coming; it seemed like the thing to do at the time. The night before the Pope came to Galway we had a wild party in Gary's house; well, it was fairly raucous by our standards. It petered out at around three or four in the morning and we all walked in the dark from the party to the racecourse as the dawn came up. It was a grey, damp morning and we had a serious hangover when we saw the Pope.

In between his leaving school and taking up the Wrangler job in Galway, Gary Sheehan went back for the Leaving Cert. party. 'That was about April or May 79. It was a kind of low-rent version of the Debs. I remember Gary had his Dad's car. We all had a great night,' McNally says.

In 1982 Frank McNally applied to join the gardaí. Unknown to him, so too did Gary Sheehan. He had been made redundant from Wrangler; he then took another job, but, because of the recession, was laid off a second time.

> My impression is that joining the guards was not something he had been planning to do. Sometime in early 1983 I got called for a medical to the Phoenix Park [garda headquarters] and I met Gary there. It was the first time I

had seen him since Galway and we had a chat about things at home. He was asking was I doing much in the way of keeping fit. He was looking forward to [joining the gardaí] up to a point. I think, of all the guys in our class, Gary was the one most likely to succeed in life.

The applicants were split up: McNally and Sheehan were put into separate groups. 'Our group got called before lunch, and his was being called in the afternoon. We said goodbye and Gary said "I'll see you in Templemore."' That was the last time McNally saw his old school friend alive. 'I never knew he'd been called up until I heard … that he'd been killed at Ballinamore. In a few seconds you find out that he'd started his career as a garda and now he was dead, all in a few months.'

Garda Denis Connolly, who is now a juvenile liaison officer at Carrickmacross, coached the Carrickmacross Emmets in 1978, the year they won the Monaghan county final. Gary Sheehan was on the team. 'He was a grand lad, very outgoing. He was delighted when the team won the final that year.' Connolly was at home on 16 December when the news came through that a recruit-garda had been killed in the rescue of Don Tidey. 'I rang the station and they told me it was Gary. I'll never forget the shock. He was such a nice lad.'

Detective Jim Sheehan, Gary's father, died in November 1996. On the day of the killings he was in a Carrickmacross shop when the news of Don Tidey's release was announced: 'The happiness and relief among the people in the shop was unbelievable; they were so delighted for him and his family,' he told the *Irish Independent* that day. 'Everybody in the shop was smiling.' A local vet came in and mentioned to Sheehan that a soldier and a garda had been shot at Ballinamore. 'I said they were not badly injured; it just never struck me that I would be told later on that my son had been killed. We were very, very proud of him. He was such a happy lad and contented with what he was doing. I think it was a stupid way to die; he was the apple of his mother's eye.' Being twice made redundant had influenced his son to join the gardaí, Jim Sheehan said. 'He told me that he was not going to be made redundant for the third time and said that he wanted security.'

Gary Sheehan was buried under leaden skies six days before Christmas in the bleak cemetery at Carrickmacross. At the cemetery, his coffin was lifted nervously by six recruits from Templemore and borne to the graveside. A trailer, pulled by a garda vehicle, was laden with hundreds of floral tributes. They came from all quarters, from garda colleagues throughout the country, from business people, from Quinnsworth, and many from ordinary people stunned by the killing of two young men who were just doing their job. In Carrickmacross, the Christmas lights were switched off.

PATRICK KELLY was the first soldier to be killed in action in the Republic since the foundation of the state. His funeral in his hometown of Moate was a sad and muted occasion. His widow, Catriona, walked behind her husband's coffin with his parents. His four young sons were kept at home. No army guns were fired in salute as Private Kelly's coffin was lowered into the ground at the graveyard in Tobber where he was laid to rest. It was ironic, said the Bishop of Ardagh and Clonmacnoise, Dr Colm O'Reilly, that a soldier so involved in peace-keeping in places notorious for tensions could be at greater risk from his own countrymen in a County Leitrim wood.

The shooting dead of a garda and a soldier marked a new low in the conflict between the security forces and the IRA. The political fallout had already begun. Rumours began to surface that members of the security forces, in the confusion in Derrada Wood, may have killed Kelly and Sheehan. Such rumours were later proved to be false, but the secrecy surrounding the forensic details of the shootings did nothing to dampen them. (It was more than a month later before gardaí released the bare details of the ballistics reports. The RUC normally released such information between twenty-four and forty-eight hours after similar incidents.) There was criticism inside and outside the Dáil about pitting young, untrained recruits against battle-hardened IRA men. Some of it was dismissed as ill-founded, given that Patrick Kelly, an armed and experienced soldier, had died alongside Gary Sheehan. But, eighteen years on, some senior gardaí still have misgivings about sending in raw recruits. 'I don't think they should have been sent in, not when they knew who was in those woods,' one senior garda told this author.

ON SUNDAY, 18 December, six men including John Joe McGirl, Joe McGirl and Hugh Prior, were released from garda custody without charge. One of the kidnappers had escaped the garda cordon on the Friday night and another three got away in the Drumshanbo direction on the Sunday. The search for the kidnappers was a sight to behold: Ballinamore and the surrounding area took on the appearance of a garrison town in wartime. Not since the Civil War had the country seen anything like it. Mobilisation began at dawn on the morning after the killings. Hundreds of heavily armed troops and gardaí threw a security drag-net six square miles around the woods at Derrada,

Ardmoneen and Aughnasheelan village. On the Sunday afternoon, Chief Superintendent J.J. McNally emerged from a conference room thinking aloud. 'The feckers are up there somewhere but how do I get them out?'

Despite public assertions to the contrary, garda and army officers were admitting privately that the search was a dead duck. Too much time had elapsed in the first few hours when darkness was falling. The gang was long gone. The Air Corps' lack of sophisticated equipment for long-range and night flying didn't help matters. Morale was low and nerves shredded. One young garda surveying the bog and scrubland near Ballinamore remarked: 'God, now I know what Cromwell meant when he said "To Hell or to Connacht".' During the Ardmoneen Wood flush-out a soldier said to a reporter: 'Those guys don't want to be taken alive and we're not interested in taking them alive.' At a checkpoint at Ardmoneen, a garda officer ordered three reporters and a photographer to leave: 'You can't follow any further. I can't accept responsibility for what might happen.' Turning to his men, he shouted: 'Right, men, into the wood — go!' One reporter persisted. A young garda reached underneath his raincoat and, pulling out a snub-nosed .38 revolver, pushed it through the open window and told the reporter he would be well advised to back off and go back to where he had come from.

The first time the gardaí publicly admitted their disappointment was on Christmas Eve. 'We are bitterly disappointed that they have got away,' said Superintendent Vincent Smyth, co-ordinator of the search. 'They could now be in Belfast. We are satisfied they either escaped from the area before we had a chance to cordon it off or else slipped through the cordons during the night.'

At the time, gardaí let it be known that they wanted to

question four men in particular: a McAlistair, McDonnell, McKiernan and Brendan (Bik) McFarlane, the leader of the IRA prisoners at the Maze Prison during the 1983 breakout and in whom the RUC also had a special interest. During the next decade and a half, gardaí in charge of the search operation would spend a lot of time thinking about the men who had got away.

Hugh Prior, the prisoner who was shot in his own car, sued the gardaí for lack of duty of care. He was awarded £30,000 compensation against the state for his injuries. 'He was the net beneficiary of the whole thing,' was the rueful comment of one former officer.

Two years after the kidnapping, a prominent IRA man from Cork, Michael Burke, walked into Tralee Garda Station and asked the gardaí if they had been looking for him. In a subsequent identity parade, a witness to the kidnapping picked Burke out as one of the men who had posed as gardaí on the morning Don Tidey was kidnapped. Burke was convicted of false imprisonment in June 1986 and sentenced to twelve years.

After the Ballinamore affair, Brendan McFarlane fled to Amsterdam. It was there that the RUC finally caught up with him. He was extradited to Northern Ireland and was returned to the Maze on 3 December 1986 but was released on parole in 1997. On 6 January 1998 McFarlane was due to sign papers granting his full release. He had just arrived back in Ireland having spent Christmas and the New Year in Copenhagen with his Danish girlfriend. He was on a bus travelling northwards to sign the papers when it stopped at a permanent garda checkpoint on the main Dublin to Belfast road. Garda headquarters had alerted the Dundalk gardaí that a man fitting McFarlane's description was on the bus. They took him from the bus and he was brought under heavy security to the Special Criminal Court in Dublin, where he was charged with falsely imprisoning Donald James Tidey between 25 November and 16 December 1983 and possession of a firearm with intent to endanger life at Derrada Wood between the same dates.

McFarlane was freed on £100,000 bail pending a full trial. After having served a total of nineteen and a half years in jail, it was now his intention to live a normal life, he told the court. 'And if that [another trial] is part and parcel of it I must face my responsibilities.' Subsequently McFarlane sought a judicial review of his case. He is due back in the Special Criminal Court in October 2001.

10

Detective Garda
Frank Hand

⁂

At 7.25 a.m. on 10 August 1984, post office van driver James Bell and his helper, Donal Brady, set off from the central sorting office in Dublin city centre on 'Route 3'. There were twenty-three mailbags on board containing almost £300,000 in cash, mostly social welfare and pension money. The mailbags were due to be dropped off at nineteen sub post offices along the route.

Route 3 began at Dunboyne in County Meath, then on to Batterstown and Drumree and back through Blanchardstown, Cabra and Phibsboro. The last stop was Berkeley Road, not far from O'Connell Street.

As the van pulled off, an unmarked garda car, a light beige Fiat Mirafiori 1600, drew in behind it. Detective Garda Frank Hand, from the Central Detective Unit in Harcourt Square, was driving. Detective Garda Michael Dowd from the Special Branch was beside him in the passenger seat. Just before 7 a.m., Dowd had signed out an attaché case with an Uzi sub-machine-gun from the garda Dublin headquarters at Harcourt Square. He was now putting the case, containing three magazines carrying twenty rounds each, on the back seat. He put another magazine into the Uzi and left another on the floor of the car at his feet. He was also armed with a Walther semi-automatic pistol.

Frank Hand was armed with a .38 Smith and Wesson revolver. At twenty-six, he had been a detective for three years and had been assigned to the Central Detective Unit that spring. Each week, sixty or seventy Central Detective Unit detectives were assigned to escort duty, working alongside Special Branch detectives. Detective Hand worked mainly on serious crime, only occasionally carrying out mail van duty. The previous day, he had been rostered for post office duty starting at 7 a.m. on 10 August. He was in good spirits that summer morning as he set off behind the post office van on Route 3. He was only a week back from his honeymoon in Venice with Bangharda Breda Hogan and the couple had set up home at Hillcrest Heights, in Lucan, County Dublin.

The two detectives stayed a hundred yards or so behind James Bell's van. The first stop was Dunboyne, just beyond the Meath–Dublin border. Detective Dowd sat in the car, his Uzi on his lap, monitoring approaching vehicles for anything suspicious. The post office helper, Donal Brady, got out of the van and picked up a mailbag. James Bell stayed at the wheel. Frank Hand got out of the garda car and walked with Brady to the door of the post office. Hand rapped on the door of the post office and Brady handed over the bag.

Batterstown was the next stop. Same procedure: Hand and Brady went to the door, Dowd and Bell stayed put. Dowd saw nothing suspicious. Brady handed over the Batterstown cash delivery. It was approximately 7.50 a.m. There was now £202,900 in the van. The next stop was Drumree.

Drumree is a tiny village twenty miles north of Dublin and

about forty miles south of Dundalk. There is a lay-by at Drumree Post Office behind a small stone wall. To the left is a narrow laneway. The post office is part of Gilsenan's public house and small grocery shop about two miles from Dunshaughlin on the road to Trim. James Bell steered his van into the lay-by, making a hairpin turn to the right and stopping with the passenger door right opposite the door of the post office. The garda Fiat coasted to a stop about six feet behind the van.

Michael Gilsenan, the postmistress's son, was preparing to receive the mailbag delivery. It was exactly 8.03 a.m. Donal Brady grabbed a couple of mailbags from the front seat of the van and headed for the post office door. Two gunmen crouching behind the wall of the Gilsenans' tiny garden were watching him. As Brady went into the post office, the gunmen rushed through the garden gate. They were wearing dark blue boiler suits, black gloves and balaclavas with red stitching around the mouths. The man in front was armed with a Sten sub-machine-gun; the other was holding a .455 calibre Webley revolver.

Michael Dowd caught the sudden movement just as the gunmen were opening fire. He shouted to Frank Hand, but his warning was drowned by a gunman shouting 'Get down you fucker!' Then the shooting started. The gunman with the Webley fired three shots. Two bullets hit the rear left door of the garda car and one passed through the car, missing both detectives and smashing through the driver's window beside Frank Hand. The gunman pulled the trigger again but the two rounds misfired. The gunman with the sub-machine-gun was now moving to the front left of the Fiat. He fired a burst of automatic fire at the two detectives, either in one single burst of eight shots or in two rapid bursts of four shots. Four bullets hit the windscreen, ripping the chrome and rubber strip holding the glass. One of them ripped across the dashboard and lodged in the driver's door, now hanging open. One of the raiders was shouting 'Out, Out.' Michael Dowd felt a stinging pain in the side of his head where a sliver of metal from a fragmented bullet had grazed his forehead on the right side. He lifted his hand to his head and slumped over the passenger seat, his Uzi slipping from his lap.

Frank Hand was halfway out of the driver's door when the shooting started, his Smith and Wesson in his hand. He fired two shots, one hitting the post office wall seven feet from the ground. Two more bullets from the Sten hit the Fiat's windscreen and a seventh hit the window of the driver's door. The eighth, and last, bullet got Frank Hand in the upper right chest and travelled down through his body, causing profuse bleeding. He spun around, falling face down towards the back of the car.

Michael Dowd was still struggling when one of the gunmen pulled the door open and put a gun to his head; his Walther semi-automatic pistol was pulled from its holster. He was pulled by the arm out of the car and pushed onto his hands and knees. 'On your belly,' the gunman ordered. The radio was ripped from the dash.

James Bell was still at the wheel of the post office van. The man with the sub-machine-gun ordered him to 'Turn off the fucking ignition.' 'For God's sake stop shooting, there's a man dead,' someone was shouting. Bell switched off the ignition, pulled out the keys and held them in his right hand. A beige Opel Ascona and a red Mercedes swept into the lay-by and skidded to a halt outside the post office. James Bell was ordered to open the back door of the van. The mailbags were propped up against the inside wall of the van. Bell was now lying on the ground face down. One of the gunmen held a gun to the back of his neck. 'If you move son, you are fucking dead,' he warned.

Michael Dowd, still lying on the ground, turned his head slightly to the right. He saw his colleague Frank Hand on the ground bleeding and what he thought were eight gunmen. The leader of the gang was giving orders in a Northern accent. 'Shoot him, shoot him,' he said several times to the raider standing next to Dowd. The postmistress, Mary Gilsenan, was in the family house, some sixty yards away, when she heard the shots. She rang the post office. Michael Gilsenan and Donal Brady had been chatting when they heard the crackle of gunfire. Michael shouted 'Dial 999'. Then a gunman entered the post office and slammed down the phone.

Out front, the gunmen began frantically transferring the mailbags from the van to the Mercedes and the Opel Ascona. As they were ready to leave the scene, the leader shouted: 'If that fucking bastard moves, fucking shoot him — shoot him.' Four of the gunmen jumped into the Opel. The remaining gunmen got into the Mercedes, which reversed and sped off towards Trim. Michael Dowd looked across at James Bell. Both men were still on the ground and it was deadly quiet. 'Are they all gone?' Dowd asked. Donal Brady came out to the van. 'Are you all right J.J.?' he said to Bell. Michael Dowd looked under the car to where Frank Hand was lying face down in a large pool of blood beside the driver's door. 'Are you all right, Frank?' Dowd whispered. There was no response.

The entire raid had lasted about three minutes, and at the end of it Frank Hand was dead. The Opel took off in the direction of Dunshaughlin, turning left just before the village onto a short link road near Skreen, at a place called Grange End. The Mercedes headed for Skreen and at the third crossroads turned left and drove for three-quarters of a mile before coming to a stop in a field at Rathfeigh. It was parked close to a ten-foot high hedge, hidden from the road. The gunmen poured petrol over the Mercedes and set it alight. Within seconds, it was an inferno. The mass of flames rose in the early morning sun and the smoke was spotted half a mile away.

By 8.30 a.m., when RTÉ broke the news of a robbery at Drumree, the raiders had ditched the cars used in the robbery, transferred the money and the guns to getaway cars and were speeding north, towards Drogheda.

FRANK HAND was killed ten days before his twenty-seventh birthday. He was born in County Roscommon, one of seven children — four boys and three girls — of Michael and Theresa Hand. His parents had a small holding in Ardmullen, outside Curraghboy. His three sisters and one of his brothers worked as teachers in Dublin. As a child he had attended the local primary school and St Aloysius College in Athlone.

Frank Hand joined the gardaí in 1977 and was always based in Dublin; he was stationed at Donnybrook and Irishtown before moving on to the drugs squad and then to the Central Detective Unit in Harcourt Square. He was an outgoing man, and well liked by his colleagues. His wife of five weeks, Breda Hogan, also worked there, in the fraud squad. From Ballinasloe, County Galway, Breda joined the gardaí in November 1978 and was stationed at Store Street and the Bridewell in Dublin before moving on to Harcourt Square.

Frank Hand's body was brought home to the small church at Kiltoom, near his parents' farm at Curraghboy. A post-mortem had been carried out at Our Lady's Hospital, Navan, about ten miles from the spot where the killing took place. Dr Kieran Cuddihy, a Waterford pathologist, found that death had been caused by haemorrhage and asphyxia from the passage of a bullet through the chest.

Hundreds of cars followed the cortège on the journey from Navan to Kiltoom, where a crowd of five thousand mourners were waiting. Along the route through Athboy, Delvin, Mullingar, Moate and Athlone, people stood in silence as the tricolour-draped coffin passed. Outside the church in Kiltoom, hundreds knelt on the gravel and prayed.

Along the mile from the church to the cemetery, the Garda Band played 'Coming Home' in the bright August sunshine. The tiny cemetery at Kiltoom is set among lush meadows and looks down on the magnificent sweep of Lough Ree. It is just a few miles away from the Hand family home. Michael Dowd placed a wreath on the coffin beside the red rose placed there by Breda Hogan. 'We had a lifetime of happiness in those five full weeks,' she had said about her short marriage. At the time of his murder, she was pregnant with their first child. She would later give birth to a daughter.

Among the dignitaries who attended the state funeral was Feargal Quinn, chairman of An Post. Almost immediately after the murder An Post had offered a reward of £50,000 for information leading to the capture of the gang that had killed Frank Hand. The Taoiseach, Garret FitzGerald, was on a family holiday in France when he got news of the murder. He returned home. On the day of the funeral, 13 August, he arrived at the Athlone home of the Fine Gael Minister for Defence, Patrick Cooney, for an emergency ministerial meeting to discuss the security crisis surrounding the Hand murder. The Tánaiste, Dick Spring, was already there; so too were the Minister for Foreign Affairs, Peter Barry, the Minister for Justice, Michael Noonan, and the Attorney General, Peter Sutherland. The Garda

Commissioner, Larry Wren, and the Army Chief of Staff, Gerry O'Sullivan, briefed the cabinet members.

The ministers were alarmed at the apparent ease with which heavily armed gardaí had been ambushed. They questioned the methods used by the security forces in providing protection for large amounts of cash. They raised the absence of army protection for what amounted to 'banks on wheels' at a time when the IRA was attempting to replenish dwindling funds. In 1984, more than 130,000 old age pensions were paid in post offices each week. The ministers also questioned the wisdom of using an ordinary post office van to transport almost £300,000. After the meeting, Garret FitzGerald announced that army backup for gardaí escorting large amounts of cash and other high-risk deliveries would now be mandatory.

Two weeks after the Athlone meeting, it emerged that senior garda officers had been warned that Drumree Post Office was vulnerable to attack. No additional precautions were put in place up to the time Frank Hand was shot dead. The warning was contained in an internal garda memorandum dated 29 September 1983 and was sent by a sergeant in the Central Detective Unit to his superior officers. Specifically, the memo warned against the dangers of delivering large amounts of cash in ordinary post office vans. Significantly, it mentioned the extraordinary practice whereby vanloads of cash made their first deliveries to post offices farthest from Dublin, thereby leaving the consignment vulnerable for the greatest length of time. It listed a number of post offices north and south of Dublin considered to be at risk. The first on the list was Drumree.

The outward journey of the post office van on Route 3 — through Phibsboro and Blanchardstown — was the route it would take back to Dublin, dropping off cash along the way. It made little sense because the van was going to one of the most distant points on the route before it began dropping off mailbags. It was exactly the scenario warned against in the memo. Had the van begun offloading cash at post offices on its way out of the city, it would have arrived at Drumree with just a couple of thousand pounds on board.

On the night of 21 August, about 150 gardaí from the Central Detective Unit, Special Branch and other armed divisions met Deputy Garda Commissioner Paul McMahon at Harcourt Square. It was an emotional affair, with various speakers, including colleagues of Frank Hand, demanding an explanation of why the suggestions in the September memorandum had not led to immediate changes in the system. They were told that, because An Post was unwilling to change its system of delivery, the garda authorities felt that they had no option but to accept.

Frank Hand's death was to change all that. Within days of the murder, An Post altered its delivery system. It also announced the introduction of a new credit card system of payment for pensioners and other social welfare recipients. The era of plastic welfare money was about to dawn.

As the politicians were issuing statements of sympathy, shock and outrage, a murder investigation got under way. Within hours of the killing, hundreds of armed and unarmed gardaí, supported by soldiers, descended on County Meath, setting up checkpoints at the county border and conducting house-to-house enquiries. Six spent bullets — the nine-millimetre parabellum type, similar to those found in other armed robberies — were discovered at the scene. The prime suspect was the Provisional IRA.

A great deal of attention was paid to the stolen cars that had been used in the robbery. The red Mercedes was quickly identified as one stolen in Newry, County Down, on 27 July. It had belonged to John Small of Newcastle. He had parked it in a car park on Monaghan Street, near the Cupid Nightclub in Newry; when he returned to pick it up, it was missing. Exactly three months earlier, a retired garda had been on a night out at the golf club in Salthill, County Galway. He parked his beige Opel Ascona in the car park. When he returned to the car park at 1.30 a.m. the Ascona was gone. His cheque-book, banker's card, briefcase, golf equipment and documents relating to the Ascona were also missing. The briefcase was handed in to Coolock Garda Station in Dublin two days later. The cheque-book and other documents were still missing.

Tommy Eccles was a twenty-four-year-old Provo from Grange Road, Muirhevnamore, in Dundalk, a large working-class housing estate on the left side of the main Dublin to Belfast road. Dundalk had, and still has, a large Northern population. Thousands of nationalists fled across the border to escape the loyalist pogroms that prevailed throughout the summer of 1969 and into 1970. Some settled permanently in Muirhevnamore. Eccles, an unemployed glazier, had been instructed by the Provos to go to Newry to pick up the red Mercedes. He found the car parked near the nightclub with the keys in the ignition. He drove it south of the border to Dromiskin, to the home of a landscape gardener called Paddy Duffy. Duffy, a republican sympathiser, had also been given the Opel Ascona for safe-keeping a few months before. He hid both cars on a farm near Castlebellingham. The Provos had earmarked the stolen cars for the Drumree robbery, along with two 'legit' cars, a blue Ford Cortina and a yellow Ford Escort.

Joe Gargan, a thirty-four-year-old lorry driver and former

Sinn Féin branch chairman from Kentstown, County Meath, owned the Escort. Noel McCabe, a Provo sympathiser from Oliver Plunkett Park, Dundalk, had done repairs to the Cortina but he did not return it immediately to its owner. Instead, he began driving it himself. Four cars were now ready for the Drumree raid.

McCabe was a bit of a fixer. He also had a problem with alcohol, but in August 1984, he was off the drink. To keep his mind occupied, he would tinker with broken television sets and other electrical goods in his garden shed. Sometime in 1983, a man from Northern Ireland arrived at McCabe's house with a television set that needed repairs. His nickname was Benny. McCabe fixed the set. Benny returned in February 1984 and the two got chatting; over time, they struck up a friendship. Eventually, Benny asked McCabe if he was up to doing a bit of work for the Provos. McCabe agreed.

At first, he fixed walkie-talkies but before long, he found himself driving the Provos around. This entailed picking people up, dropping them off at a certain location and calling back for them a few hours later. The Provos paid him petrol money. One of his regular 'pick-ups' was a Northern man he used to see around Dundalk. McCabe was told to pass him by if he ever saw him in the street. There are two types of IRA personnel: the activists, those who carry out the operations; and the 'ancillaries', those who supply the necessary logistical backup. McCabe became a solid member of the second group. The more McCabe stayed in the background, and out of the eye of the security forces, the more valuable he was to the Provos, initially as a driver and then as a weapons courier.

In the late spring of 1984, the IRA began leaving guns with McCabe. The first was a .38 automatic revolver and then a sawn-off shotgun. He hid them in his shed, underneath a workbench. But he was worried: driving Provos around was one thing — stashing guns in his shed was another. McCabe was getting jittery, and the IRA knew it. They asked him to do one last run, to bring Benny to a meeting and then drop him back to Dundalk. McCabe agreed.

He didn't hear from the Provos again until early July when Benny arrived with a sackload of guns, containing two carbines, a Sten gun, a pistol and an old revolver. 'Headquarters know you held guns for us before,' Benny told McCabe, leaving him in no doubt that the Provos expected no resistance from him. McCabe was aghast but he put them under the workbench, as before. In early August, the Provos removed them, but they again asked McCabe to go back on chauffeur duty. This time, he was to drive Benny to an old farmhouse near Carrickmacross in County Monaghan. While they were there, another two cars pulled into the yard and Benny began passing rifles to the drivers. Noel McCabe dropped him back to Dundalk and, on the way, he was told he had another assignment. This time, he was to pick up three men the following Friday morning and take them to Dundalk. On the Thursday night, 9 August, he would be given instructions about the pick-up point.

Noel McCabe may or may not have been aware that the IRA had had Drumree Post Office under observation for at least three weeks before the raid. Benny, the Northern Ireland man, was the leader of the IRA unit that planned and carried out a number of robberies in the Meath–Louth area, including Drumree. On the night of 9 August he was putting in place the final preparations for the Drumree robbery. He had gone to Drogheda at midday and met a republican named Seamus Lynch. He drove Lynch to the field at Rathfeigh and told him to make sure he was there at 8 a.m. the following morning.

Paddy Duffy was standing by with the stolen cars. Tommy Eccles would drive the Mercedes to the scene of the robbery. Two other men, Brian McShane, from Dundalk, and Pat McPhillips, a native of Lurgan, County Armagh, but now living in Dundalk, would help offload the cash into the Mercedes. Noel McCabe was to be a getaway driver, driving three of the robbers to safety in the blue Cortina. That Thursday night, McCabe drove Benny to Paddy Duffy's yard at Dromiskin, where the cars and guns were assembled. He showed McCabe the crossroads where he was to pick up the raiders the following morning and gave him £30 for petrol. Eccles, McShane and McPhillips travelled in the stolen cars from Duffy's yard to a shed near Dunshaughlin, some three miles from Drumree Post Office. Everything was now in place.

Noel McCabe left Dundalk at 7.10 a.m. on 10 August in the Cortina. He headed south-west towards the crossroads at Dunshaughlin. Seamus Lynch had been up from dawn and was now heading towards the field at Rathfeigh, as instructed, in Joe Gargan's Escort. Two armed men had positioned themselves in the laneway beside Drumree Post Office waiting for James Bell's van to arrive. It was just before 8 a.m.

Five minutes later, as Frank Hand was lying dead, McCabe was waiting at the crossroads in the Cortina. Lynch was pulling into the designated spot in the field at Rathfeigh. Eccles was now speeding away from Drumree in the Mercedes on his way to Rathfeigh, past McCabe. McCabe took off after him and they all met in Rathfeigh. There, all hell broke loose. No one had expected a garda to be shot dead. There was panic in the field. Arguing broke out as they were dumping the money, guns, boiler suits and walkie-talkies into the boot of the Escort. The Mercedes was set alight. Lynch drove the Escort towards Kentstown, and Eccles, McPhillips and another raider got into

McCabe's Cortina and sped off towards Drogheda. The Opel Ascona had disappeared, with Benny and some of the guns in it. McCabe knew something had gone badly wrong. 'What happened?' he asked. 'Shut up. Just drive,' McPhillips shouted. He was pale from shock and panic.

They got lost in the narrow roads. At Julianstown, about four miles out of Drogheda, Noel McCabe ordered McPhillips and the other raider out of the car. McPhillips was in no state to argue. McCabe drove Eccles to Drogheda and then continued on to Dundalk, where he went to Mass before returning home. Tommy Eccles went into St Peter's Church in Drogheda, and thanked God that he had escaped safely. He walked nonchalantly around the shops for a while, and then took a taxi home to Muirhevnamore around lunchtime. On the way he heard on the news that a garda had been shot dead at Drumree. While this was going on, Lynch was driving the guns and the money to a shed about a mile from Kentstown, where Joe Gargan was waiting. They hid the lot in an empty oil tank, went home and lay low.

Two days later, Noel McCabe went to Tommy Eccles' house. Benny, the Northern man, was already there. McCabe still wanted to know what had gone wrong: killing a garda was not part of the plan. 'It went wrong,' said Benny; 'we didn't mean to shoot anyone. I didn't intend to involve you in anything like this.' But McCabe was involved in what was now capital murder. If caught and convicted, he knew he could hang.

Noel McCabe would probably not have known that the 'no warning' shooting of Detective Frank Hand and the wounding of Detective Michael Dowd at Drumree was the manifestation of a changed policy within the Provisional IRA. Exactly one year earlier, armed detectives had shot and wounded four IRA men in a shoot-out in Roundwood, County Wicklow, following an abortive kidnap attempt on millionaire businessman Galen Weston (see Chapter 9). The IRA claimed that their men had been fired on without warning. After that, the organisation decided to take no chances in possible confrontations with armed gardaí. The killing of Frank Hand at Drumree was partly the result of that new policy, but also partly due to panic. At the time, the Drumree raid was portrayed as a well-planned robbery. In fact, it was badly organised, poorly carried out and dependent on amateurs like Noel McCabe and Tommy Eccles. The net result was the killing of an innocent man.

McCabe was numb with shock and overcome with remorse over what had happened. He turned to a Redemptorist priest, Fr McAuley, and confessed his part in the robbery. He told the priest that he wanted to tell someone else as well. Fr McAuley thought that would be a very wise decision. It would be two weeks before Noel McCabe got around to telling anyone else. And by that stage the game was up.

On 13 August gardaí began rounding up known Provisionals. During the routine round-up they called to the homes of Seamus Lynch and Joe Gargan, who were both living in Oliver Plunkett Park in Kentstown. Gargan was very talkative but was short on answers about his whereabouts on the day of the murder. Both men, truthfully, placed themselves miles away from the scene of the shooting (Lynch was in Rathfeigh while Gargan was in Kentstown).

Detectives began to look closely at the Kentstown area. A local woman had noticed a truck driving up to a barn about fifteen minutes after the Drumree robbery and she reported it to the gardaí. Other people in the area remembered trucks coming and going at odd hours of the night. Shortly after midnight on

15 August, gardaí based in several Dublin stations were roused from their beds and told to report to garda headquarters in Phoenix Park at 5.30 a.m. They were going to Navan. Shortly after dawn, hundreds of armed detectives and troops descended on the Brownstown and Kentstown area of Meath. Every road leading to the area was sealed off as detectives surrounded a large barn at the end of a narrow lane. The main entrance was through two large sliding doors with a small door cut into one of them. It was 10 a.m. before they located a key and got inside.

They went straight to a disused tank that had been converted into a container. They climbed a ladder leading to the tank, and several feet up one of the walls, they found orange post office bags hidden inside a large grey post office sack containing the £202,900 taken at Drumree. The Uzi sub-machine-gun taken from Detective Michael Dowd was also hidden there, along with handguns, an assault rifle and walkie-talkies. It took fifteen bags to remove the haul. The Minister for Justice, Michael Noonan, was at a cabinet meeting in Dublin when news of the breakthrough was flashed to him.

Six men were arrested that morning under section 30 of the Offences Against the State Act, including Lynch and Gargan. While detectives were turning Lynch's home inside out, he made a statement admitting his part in the robbery. The suspects were now beginning to crumble. The following evening, Lynch and Gargan were charged with the robbery of £202,900 at Drumree Post Office. They were brought from Navan under heavy garda and army escort to the non-jury Special Criminal Court in Dublin's Green Street, arriving there at 9.43 p.m. The special sitting lasted thirty-five minutes. Armed troops stood guard outside.

Paddy Duffy was now becoming increasingly anxious. He was

in bed when the gardaí came for him at 6.20 a.m. on 22 August. He was taken to Navan while gardaí searched his house, finding guns and counterfeit money. Detective sergeants Kevin Carty and Patrick Lynagh interviewed Duffy. He told them he knew nothing about the robbery, had never heard of Drumree and wouldn't know how to get there. 'I've never stood in it in my life,' he said. As the day wore on, his attitude changed and he began to talk. Duffy made a statement admitting his own role in the robbery. He also owned up to the weapons and counterfeit money found in his home. The detectives asked him to 'name names'.

'You better get me a hundred thousand and a fast plane if you want me to do something like that,' Duffy replied. He answered questions, admitting that he kept stolen cars for the IRA but denied knowing that a garda was going to be shot in the robbery. 'I thought the cars were going to be used in the North for use against the British army,' he said. Duffy was brought to Green Street at 5.20 p.m. and was rushed into the courthouse, handcuffed to a detective. He was in a holding cell waiting to be charged with the murder of Frank Hand when detectives again asked him to name names. 'When I saw the capital murder charge, the wind was taken out of me,' he later told the court.

Tommy Eccles had been arrested around the same time as Paddy Duffy. He denied knowing anything about the Drumree murder. 'I would rather go to Portlaoise for forty years than have it said I made a statement,' he told detectives. After a visit from his solicitor, who told him his wife had been arrested, Eccles fell apart. He was now prepared to admit his own involvement, but he would not be naming any names. 'I'm not a hard man; I'm not bullshitting you. I went into a church and said a prayer for that garda after the robbery. Only for my wife and kids I'd have skipped it,' he said. Eccles made a signed statement. He was then taken to the Special Criminal Court and charged with the capital murder of Detective Frank Hand.

Noel McCabe was a nervous wreck. On Thursday, 23 August, the day after Eccles and Duffy were charged, he rang Brendan McGahon, the Fine Gael TD for Louth. McGahon knew McCabe and was aware of his drink problem. That Friday night McCabe arrived at McGahon's house and told him about his role in the robbery. He stayed for three hours, talking. When he left, McGahon rang the gardaí. McCabe went to an Alcoholics Anonymous meeting on Sunday night, returning to McGahon's home on the Monday. The deputy was not at home. The gardaí, however, had contacted McGahon at his Dáil office. Between 6.25 and 6.45 a.m. on 29 August Noel McCabe, Brian McShane and Pat McPhillips were all arrested. Ten minutes after being taken to Navan Garda Station, Noel McCabe began making a detailed and convincing confession. He told the gardaí everything he knew about the robbery. He corroborated elements of statements made earlier by other members of the gang. McCabe wanted to get it all 'off his chest'.

Brian McShane and Pat McPhillips made statements in custody which they would later claim were neither voluntary nor true. In his statement, McShane said he was part of a gang who had been 'given guns and orders' near Drumree Post Office the night before Frank Hand was shot dead. The guns were put into a car that was 'going on a job'. The gang leader said 'there would be Special Branch with the van. He handed out guns to us and gave each of us our orders. He said there were a couple of boys at the post office already staking out the place. The man told us that if the branch went for their guns that we knew what to do.' McShane admitted loading bags into a getaway car and moving out. 'My conscience is clear; I didn't shoot the garda,' he said.

On the night of 29 August, Brian McShane and Pat McPhillips were charged with capital murder. Their contested statements would later be admitted in evidence. There would also be allegations of garda beatings that was found by the court to have no substance. Noel McCabe, 'the fixer' who had got in way over his head, was charged with the robbery of £202,900 at Drumree Post Office. McCabe spent six weeks in solitary confinement in Portlaoise Prison. He pleaded guilty to the robbery charge and was remanded for sentencing.

On 20 February 1985, Tommy Eccles, Brian McShane, Pat McPhillips and Paddy Duffy stood trial for the capital murder of Frank Hand. The case was to last five weeks and the men faced a mandatory death sentence on conviction. On 28 March, the court found Eccles, McShane and McPhillips guilty of capital murder. Paddy Duffy was found guilty of non-capital murder and was sentenced to penal servitude for life. There was no evidence in Duffy's case to establish beyond reasonable doubt that he knew the exact details of the plan or that the post office van was to be escorted by gardaí.

'Stand please,' Mr Justice Liam Hamilton, presiding, said to Eccles, McShane and McPhillips. 'You have been found guilty of the crime of capital murder. The sentence and judgment of this court is that you be now removed from this court to the prison in which you were last confined, and be there detained in custody and that on Thursday, 18 April 1985, you suffer death by execution in the manner prescribed by law and that after each sentence is carried into effect your body be buried within the precincts of the prison.'

The three men remained impassive as the death sentence was imposed. Their friends and relatives looked on from the public gallery above. The four were led from the dock to the cells below, smiling and waving. Seamus Lynch pleaded guilty to robbery and was sentenced to four years' imprisonment. Joe Gargan also pleaded guilty to robbery and was given ten years, suspended. Gargan broke down in the dock when the court imposed the suspended sentence.

Then it was Noel McCabe's turn to be sentenced. He got a ten-year sentence, suspended, on condition that he have no further dealings with subversive organisations. McCabe was nodding his head in agreement with the conditions and was about to leave the dock when a man began shouting and jumping up and down in the public gallery. He was Eoin McKenna, a brother-in-law of Pat McPhillips.

'McCabe, you're only a supergrass — the first Free State supergrass,' he roared.

'Arrest that man,' the judge ordered.

'Supergrass, supergrass,' the man continued to shout, as a number of gardaí pounced on him. They dragged McKenna down the stone steps from the public gallery to the dock. He struggled all the way.

'What have you to say?' the judge demanded.

'I want to say that I have been listening here for the past four weeks. Two of the accused are innocent; the trial has been set up against them.'

'Apologise to the court.'

'How can I apologise with the likes of this going on?'

'You are sentenced to twelve months for contempt of court,' the judge retorted.

McKenna was taken to Portlaoise Prison, where he cooled his heels for three days before purging his contempt. Eccles, McShane and McPhillips appealed the death sentences. Their appeals were dismissed on 10 February 1986. Eleven days later, their sentences were commuted to forty years without remission. They were released on 22 and 23 December 1998 under the terms of the Good Friday Agreement, having served fourteen years in prison. Benny, the Northern Ireland man, left the country for a while but has since returned. The gardaí have no evidence against him for the Drumree raid. Breda Hand remained in the gardaí and is now a detective sergeant attached to the National Bureau of Criminal Investigation in Harcourt Square, Dublin.

11

Garda Sergeant Patrick Morrissey

I t started with the robbery of £25,000 and ended with the cold-blooded execution of a garda sergeant near a field of barley in the County Louth countryside. Of all the garda killings, the murder of Sergeant Paddy Morrissey on 27 June 1985 was probably the most callous and calculated. It began just before 10 o'clock on that sunny Thursday morning. Seán Boyle, the manager of Ardee Labour Exchange, had been up early that day to go to the bank. He had withdrawn enough cash from the Bank of Ireland to distribute at the exchange throughout the day. He put the money into one bag, placed it in the back of his car, and then went to pick up his daughter, Paula, who also worked at the exchange. Boyle would normally have divided the money into two separate bags, but that morning he decided to put the cash into one container, for convenience. Thursdays were usually busy at Ardee; it was one of the biggest payout days of the week.

Directly across from the exchange was an old monastery, bordered by thick bushes and trees and a high wall. The health board had taken it over and had converted it into an old folks' home. On the Wednesday night, two men had dug a trench behind the wall, covered themselves with branches and slept there. They wore masks and combat gear and were armed with a rifle, a sawn-off shotgun and a semi-automatic pistol. The gunmen were watching Boyle's Datsun as it pulled up outside the door of the labour exchange at 9.58 a.m. The manager was barely out of the car when one of them scaled the high limestone wall in front of the home and rushed at him. The first thing Boyle noticed was someone pushing him in the side.

'Money, money,' a voice said.

A shot rang out and Boyle spun around and saw the gunman. Then he saw his daughter lying on the footpath, uninjured but terrified. Almost paralysed with fear, Boyle pointed to his car and told the gunman that the money was in the back seat. The gunman grabbed the bag of money from the Datsun, containing £25,000 in cash. The gunman refused to believe Boyle when he told him there was only one bag. 'I'll blow your fucking head off,' he warned, and demanded the car keys. The second gunman was now covering people cowered on the footpath as the first raider pushed Seán Boyle into the labour exchange at gunpoint. Boyle handed over the wrong set of car keys. The gunman ran out and tried to start the ignition and then realised the keys didn't fit. He came back in and fired a shot at the wall, while all the time demanding more money. Boyle handed him the correct set of keys and the gunman ran out of the building for the second time, scooping up loose coins from underneath the counter on his way out.

Sergeant Paddy Morrissey had driven his own car from Collon Garda Station to Ardee for that morning's District Court sitting. Two uniformed gardaí, Peter Long and Paul Flynn, were on duty in the patrol car. They cruised by the exchange and saw the hold-up. It was 10.02 a.m., just four minutes after the raiders had struck. One of the gunmen spotted the squad car as it came to a halt outside the building. 'Police, police,' he shouted at his accomplice. One of them fired two shots at the patrol car but missed it. Ned Cluskey, who was living in the old monastery gate-lodge, had been painting his gate when he heard shots and saw people lying on the ground. As the gunmen got into Boyle's Datsun and took off at high speed, Cluskey picked up a large rock and aimed for the windscreen, but only managed to hit the side window.

They headed north, taking a secondary road towards Tallanstown, an isolated area a few miles west of Mansfieldstown. Flynn and Long sped off to the courthouse to pick up Morrissey and the three chased after the Datsun. A local postman saw the escape route and pointed the gardaí in the right direction. The gunmen drove on towards a field at Pepperstown where they had earlier hidden a motorbike. They abandoned the hijacked car and switched to the black, high-powered bike. As they were speeding down the narrow road, clutching the bag of cash, a car came up from the opposite direction, near Kieran's Cross. They crashed into it and the impact threw the car to the opposite side of the road. The bike and its riders went to the other side. The car driver, Stella Mallon, suffered head injuries. Her three-year-old daughter who was in the car was also hurt. The patrol car arrived at the scene within minutes of the crash. Long and Flynn stayed there to help while Morrissey ran after the raiders.

Both gunmen had been injured in the collision, one badly. Blood was gushing from a wound on his head. They took a clear, right-hand fork in the road towards Dundalk and tried to make off on foot. The gunmen went a few yards and tried to run up the driveway of Rathbrist House, an imposing residence in its own grounds. The owners, Hugh and Marie McDermott, had left for work earlier that morning. They had a dental practice in the town. Their three teenage children were at home. Morrissey spotted an adjoining boreen and decided to cut through into the grounds of Rathbrist House to head off the gunmen. They met face to face on the gravelled driveway. Morrissey called on them to give themselves up. One levelled his gun at the sergeant's groin and squeezed the trigger.

Sixteen-year-old Seán McDermott had been asleep in a second-floor bedroom. He awoke when he heard the commotion outside. One of the gunmen was now walking past the front of the house clutching some type of cap to his head. Blood was pouring down his shoulders. Sergeant Morrissey was lying on the ground, badly wounded. Looking out the window, McDermott watched in horror as the gunman stood over Morrissey and ordered him to get up. He was taunting him. Morrissey tried to stand but was unable to. He was almost in a sitting position, using his arms to prop himself up, when the gunman aimed his weapon. From point-blank range, he fired into Paddy Morrissey's face, which was tilted slightly backwards. The shot went straight through his cheek at an upwards angle just below his right eye and came out through the top of his skull. It caused extensive haemorrhaging and lacerations to the brain. The shot was fired at such close range that it left burn marks similar to injuries caused by explosives. Paddy Morrissey bled to death on the gravelled driveway. It was just twenty minutes since the robbery had taken place.

Seán McDermott came away from the window, almost stiff with fear. He ran into his sister's room and rang his mother's surgery. Fr Michael Downey from Tallanstown was quickly on the scene: 'The garda was stretched out on the avenue,' the priest later told a reporter. 'I gave him the last rites. Nothing could be done for he was already dead. He seemed to have wounds in the legs and in the head.'

Sergeant Morrissey's body was covered with a white sheet, with a rock at the bottom to prevent the sheet from moving in the light summer breeze. His garda cap was placed beside him. Bernadette Morrissey was working in the Moorland Restaurant in Drogheda when gardaí called to tell her that her husband had been shot dead. Knowing her husband as she did, he would never have held back in the face of danger, she told the *Irish Press*: 'He knew no fear of subversives and would not have pulled back from any task. Tragic and all as it is, I'd rather that this happened to me than that any one of my family would go out and take someone else's life. I am really happy that he was anointed at the scene.'

After they had killed Sergeant Morrissey, the gunmen made for a barley field, six hundred yards away. By now a major search was under way, involving armed detectives, troops and the Air Corps helicopter. The gunmen had left a trail of blood from the scene of the killing to the barley field where they were hiding. The gardaí followed the drops of blood and found one of them lying hidden in a ditch covered with grass and foliage. He was Noel Callan, a twenty-three-year-old car dealer from Culloville, Castleblayney, in County Monaghan. They called on him to come out but there was no response so they moved in and took him out of the hedge.

'Is the garda dead?' asked Callan.

'He is,' came the reply.

'Why did he follow us? Didn't he know he'd be shot?'

They were about two-thirds of the way down the field when Callan collapsed and had to be carried to the patrol car. He was taken to Louth County Hospital.

Shortly afterwards, gardaí found the second gunman. He was wearing a green combat jacket and had blood on his hand, face and knees and appeared dazed. He was Michael McHugh, a twenty-five-year-old motor mechanic from Clonalig, County Armagh. Both men were known to the gardaí and McHugh was also known to the RUC. He was out on bail for a previous offence in Northern Ireland and had been signing on once a week at Crossmaglen. By this stage, the gardaí had found a sawn-off shotgun, a rifle, and the semi-automatic pistol used to murder Paddy Morrissey, near the scene. When ballistics officers examined the scene they found a spent nine-millimetre cartridge embedded in the ground at the spot where Paddy Morrissey's body was lying. Another spent cartridge lay underneath the body. The killer had shot into Morrissey's face from a range of four to six inches.

Michael McHugh was taken to Dundalk Garda Station and then to Louth County Hospital, where he was treated for injuries he received in the crash. McHugh and Callan claimed to be members of the INLA. In fact, they were a pair of mavericks who had committed a string of criminal offences near the border. Earlier that year, McHugh had hijacked a fire engine and used it to ram a garda car in a joyride that covered three counties. The day after the murder, detective sergeants Kevin Carty and Patrick Lynagh went to Louth County Hospital to question McHugh. 'What's the use of asking me questions? You know we shot him,' he told them. He refused to make a written statement: 'I'm not saying any more. Leave me alone.' McHugh asked Carty if Callan was going to court that day. No, replied Carty, he was still in the hospital. 'We got some toss off that bike,' McHugh said. 'I suppose we were lucky; we should have been killed.' He asked Carty if the 'garda's people' would ever forgive him for what he had done, suggesting they would forget in time: 'I suppose they will but I won't. I'll have to live with it for the rest of my life.'

The two suspects were still in hospital when Paddy Morrissey was buried with the full honours of a state funeral. The Auxiliary Bishop of Armagh, Dr James Lennon, described the murder of the sergeant as a 'brutal and cold-blooded act'. As the coffin with Paddy Morrissey's cap on top was borne from St Mary's Church in Drogheda after requiem Mass, the Garda Choir, of which the sergeant was a former tenor, sang 'Nearer My God to Thee'. Thousands of people lined the streets of Drogheda, and the Garda Commissioner, Larry Wren, led hundreds of uniformed officers of all ranks from all over the country as the cortège made its way slowly through the town, in a final tribute to their murdered colleague. Then the cortège moved on to Paddy Morrissey's native town of Belturbet, County Cavan, where more crowds had gathered to say a final farewell. The dead sergeant was laid to rest at Drumaloe Cemetery in County Cavan, a short distance from the Fermanagh border. The hearse, bearing the tricolour, wound its way along the narrow country byroads followed by a long line of mourners.

THE COLD-BLOODED manner of Paddy Morrissey's execution shocked even the most hardened policemen who had grown used to violent death. The forty-nine-year-old garda was a popular officer and a father of four: two sons, aged twenty and eighteen, and two teenage daughters, fifteen and thirteen. He had joined the force in December 1960, serving in rural stations and at the Bridewell in Dublin before being transferred to garda headquarters in the Phoenix Park. He was promoted to the rank of sergeant in October 1974 and was in charge of the sub-aqua unit for five years. A strong swimmer, Sergeant Morrissey had once swam through dangerous currents at the Boyne estuary at Mornington, County Meath, to save a teenager whose canoe had overturned. He had been three years in Collon when he was killed. His neighbours described him as a good and kind man.

Paddy Morrissey was the twelfth garda to be killed since 1970. The day after his killing the call went up to arm more gardaí. Jack Marrinan of the Garda Representative Association said the issue of arming uniformed officers would have to be reviewed:

> This seems to be a case for the more extensive use of arms in the Gardaí ... I have always been against arming uniformed members but it seems a luxury after this outrage. Of the eleven murders of members of the force who died since the early 70s from what I can glean, this was more calculated and vicious than any other. The slaying was unnecessary ... if the sole reason for the shooting has been to effect escape, then it could have been done without brutally slaying this family man.

Morrissey's murder had also revived security concerns about cash in transit. Up to the 1980s, banks and building societies were the main targets for paramilitary robberies. In 1982, following pressure from the government, the banks set aside £5 million for extra security, including metal doors, time locks on doors and safes, surveillance cameras and the installation of 'bandit screens'. The net effect was that armed robbers switched to the 'softer' target of stealing public money in transit. As the number of bank robberies dropped, there was a corresponding rise in the number of post office raids, culminating in the murder of Detective Frank Hand at Drumree in August 1984. After the Hand killing, certain additional security measures were introduced, including Irish army backup for detectives escorting cash deliveries. It emerged, however, that troops were deployed only in situations where there was a specific threat or where cash in transit reached a certain figure. That figure was £100,000.

At the time of the Hand murder, and ten months before the killing of Sergeant Morrissey, the Association of Garda Sergeants and Inspectors had asked the Minister for Social Welfare, Barry Desmond, to pay social welfare recipients by cheque. The minister foresaw problems: the computerisation system could not cope; the banks would be unable to cope with increased demand; and postmen would be placed at risk. The result was that no action was taken, which only served to increase feelings of anger among gardaí when Paddy Morrissey was shot dead the following June. Michael Woods, Fianna Fáil's spokesperson on Justice, described the gardaí as 'sitting ducks' and said it was time to take the gloves off. But he stopped short of calling for an armed force: 'There is no need to arm the ordinary gardaí, but they need armed backup ... gardaí with responsibilities, particularly married men with children, could not be expected to man roadblocks if they did not have armed backup.'

AT 2.40 on the afternoon of 2 July doctors at Louth County Hospital discharged Michael McHugh. Physically, he was fit to leave but the gardaí were coming for him. McHugh immediately leapt back into bed and refused to leave the hospital. When arresting gardaí tried to get him out of bed, he started roaring and had to be carried from the hospital. It took five gardaí to get the struggling, pyjama-clad man into the patrol car. Back in Dundalk Garda Station gardaí handed McHugh some new clothes. He was placed in a carpeted room because he refused to stand or sit down. He complained about a pain in his leg. One detective, James Hanley, later claimed that the prisoner had sobbed on his shoulder saying: 'I might as well be dead. Oh God why did it happen to me?' Later that day, McHugh was taken to the Special Criminal Court in Dublin and charged with the capital murder of Sergeant Patrick Morrissey. Detectives had to carry him in because he refused to walk.

Six days later, Noel Callan appeared at the Special Criminal Court on the same charge. Both men were also accused of the robbery of £25,000 from Seán Boyle at Ardee Labour Exchange on 27 June. As the garda car passed through Ardee on its way to Dublin, Callan, handcuffed to detectives, said: 'It was a sad day we came here. If we never came to this place the sergeant would still be alive.' A motor-cycle escort met them on the outskirts of Dublin. Callan enquired how far it was to the court. About ten minutes, came the reply. He then asked if the press would be there and wondered if it would be possible for him to cover his head going in: 'I don't want anyone to see me for what I've done.'

That November, five months after the killing, Michael McHugh and Noel Callan stood trial for the murder of Sergeant Morrissey. They had pleaded not guilty. It was the state's case that McHugh had done the actual shooting. A pathologist's report showed that Sergeant Morrissey had died from cardiac arrest following extensive brain haemorrhaging resulting from a gunshot wound to the face. There was also a bullet wound on the back of his upper left leg, two centimetres below the groin.

Callan's counsel, Patrick MacEntee, said the evidence showed that Noel Callan was a 'passive presence' at the scene of the shooting.

McHugh's defence lawyers submitted that he had not made verbal admissions to the murder while in custody. They also claimed that McHugh had been ill-treated during his detention. McHugh had claimed that one officer had put his medical drip on full after it had been changed; that another had poked him in the throat and had twisted his left nipple; and that unidentified gardaí had lifted his hospital bed and let it drop, causing him pain. Dorothy Breathnach, a nurse at Louth County Hospital, told McHugh's counsel, Seamus Sorahan, that she had set up a drip for McHugh at around 9 p.m. on Saturday, 29 June. 'I set it up to run quite slowly. I thought it would run for six to eight hours,' she said. Two hours later, she returned to examine McHugh and saw the drip bag was 'completely empty'. The control wheel was fully open. The nurse had put it on restricted flow, as the patient was able to drink liquids. McHugh could have reached the control wheel by sitting up, Dorothy Breathnach agreed. He had not complained to her about the drip.

The two men gave totally conflicting accounts of events leading up to the shooting. Noel Callan claimed that on 26 June, the night before the murder, an INLA activist named James Burnett had approached him and asked Callan 'to do him a favour'. They had met during anti-H-Block demonstrations in Dundalk in 1981 and Burnett had stayed at Callan's house on occasion. Burnett, he said, had planned and carried out the Ardee robbery. Conveniently, James Burnett was dead: the INLA had murdered him that September during one of its countless feuds.

Callan's version of events went as follows: having agreed to the 'favour' he set off on a motorbike at 9.30 a.m. on 27 June to meet two men in a field. He did not identify the location of the field. While waiting for them, a car with two men inside crashed through the gate into the field. One of them ordered Callan to get on the pillion passenger seat and he drove off at high speed. They crashed. Callan recalled hitting his head on the road and collapsing into a ditch, and said that was the last recollection he had. 'I was in a dazed condition and the whole thing was just a blur to me.' Callan did not remember being arrested or taken to hospital and did not know a garda had been shot dead until he woke up on 4 July. His hearing appeared to have been unaffected, however, as he heard people talking about a shooting and claimed he heard a voice saying: 'When we get this Callan bastard out of here we'll shoot him.'

Michael McHugh, meanwhile, was singing a different tune. He claimed that he had left his house at seven that morning and had been on his way to Navan to fix a car. He was 'thumbing lifts and walking'. He was making his way through Tallanstown when he heard a loud bang, then a second bang. He came across a garda checkpoint and took to his heels across the fields to avoid being stopped: 'I had been on bail in Northern Ireland of £4,000 and was signing on once a week in Crossmaglen. After I had been released from Crumlin Road I was told by an RUC man that if I was arrested in the Republic I would lose my bail.' He claimed he had noticed frenzied police and army activity and saw men waving guns. He lay down in a ditch; then he heard a shout and was hauled out and arrested.

Detective Garda Joe Quinn had known Michael McHugh for a number of years. In 1979, he had offered to help him get a job. Quinn was on duty at Louth County Hospital guarding McHugh the night he was brought in. He said that he neither liked nor disliked McHugh and denied ill-treating him. Indeed, the court found that all allegations of garda ill-treatment were false. The court also accepted that any statements made by McHugh and Callan were made voluntarily.[1] Forensic evidence showed that twelve shards of glass found on McHugh's clothing matched fragments of glass from the car driven by Sheila Mallon. The court rejected Callan's story as lies and accepted the testimony of the eyewitness, Seán McDermott. The evidence against the accused was overwhelming.

On 2 December, the court found Noel Callan and Michael McHugh guilty of capital murder. 'There was an appreciable time between the firing of the shot that wounded Sergeant Morrissey and the shot that killed him,' said Mr Justice Liam Hamilton, presiding. The court was satisfied beyond all reasonable doubt that McHugh had fired the fatal shot and that he knew Morrissey was a garda on duty, as he was in uniform when he was shot. The judge said Callan was part of the common design to do anything to avoid arrest and to shoot if necessary. He had not withdrawn at any time up to the murder. He ordered both men to stand for the sentence. Callan stood. McHugh remained seated, his feet on the heavy wooden dock. Callan looked crestfallen as the death sentence was pronounced and the date of execution was set for 27 December. As they were being led from the dock, McHugh clenched his fist in the direction of the bench. 'Victory to the INLA, pro-British bastards.' Bernadette Morrissey, who had attended the trial every day, was in the public gallery above. 'I'm glad it's all over,' she said afterwards.

1   On 21 July 2001, Noel Callan lodged an appeal in the Court of Criminal Appeal on the grounds of new evidence that he claims will cast doubt on the admissibility of contested statements in his 1985 trial. The case is set for hearing in December 2001.

The death sentence was later commuted to forty years' penal servitude without remission. McHugh and Callan are not aligned to any of the paramilitary groups covered by the Good Friday Agreement, and are therefore not entitled to early release. Their release date is June 2025.

12

Detective Garda Jerry McCabe

I didn't lose consciousness; I knew that if I did, I'd bleed to death. I realised control was calling us ... on the first radio. I went to pick it up but it fell through my fingers ... I tried to turn my fingers into Jerry's wrist but there was no pulse.

Detective Garda Ben O'Sullivan

On 31 May 1996, a man parked his black Pajero jeep outside his home at Butterfield Park, Rathfarnham, in Dublin. Sometime during the night, a member of the IRA from west Dublin 'hotwired' it and drove it away. When the owner got up for work the following morning, he found that his jeep had been stolen. Five days later, on Wednesday, 5 June, a Mayo woman parked her new silver Mitsubishi Lancer at Durham Road, Sandymount, in Dublin. When she came to collect it, it was missing. That same night, the IRA stole a third car, a red Nissan Sunny, from the railway station at Thurles, County Tipperary.

John Quinn, from Faha in Patrickswell, County Limerick, was working on a building site near Ballybrown GAA club on the Wednesday. John Quinn was a Provo. A fortnight earlier, Kevin Walsh, a forty-two-year-old IRA man, had instructed Quinn to buy plastic ties for a job that was coming up. Walsh, who was also known as 'Rusty' or 'The Fox' because of his reddish-coloured hair, had given Quinn a cheque for £48. He called to see Quinn at the site that Wednesday, 5 June. He ordered Quinn to get his girlfriend's car, bring the plastic ties with him, and collect a man from the by-pass at Rathkeale, County Limerick, at 10.15 p.m. the following night. Walsh gave Quinn a description of the man. He said his name was Jerry.

At 9.30 p.m. on the Thursday, John Quinn left his girlfriend's house in her white Peugeot, went home to collect the plastic ties and headed for Rathkeale as instructed. A stocky man with a moustache was standing near a garage on the old road. As Quinn passed him by, the man glanced at him and, slowly, Quinn turned the car around. 'Are you Jerry?' he asked. The man nodded. He was Jeremiah Sheehy, a thirty-six-year-old Provo from Abbey Park in Rathkeale, who had served time for robbing a post office van in 1989. Quinn drove Sheehy to a house in Patrickswell, the home of Kevin Walsh's father, Paddy.

'You are not going on the job, or are you?' Sheehy asked along the way.

'No,' Quinn replied.

Quinn handed Sheehy the plastic ties. On the way, a Special Branch car passed them. 'Don't stop, turn left and keep going,' Sheehy ordered.

When they arrived at Patrickswell, Kevin Walsh was already there. 'We have to go on a bit of a run,' he told Quinn. They took the back roads, crossing the main Limerick road, turning left before the level crossing and arriving at Annacotty, a tiny village about five miles from Limerick on the main Dublin to

Limerick road. 'Drive on, we're running late,' Walsh ordered. As they came up to a car park outside Finnegan's pub, Walsh said: 'That's where we're having our meeting, but keep going.' They drove on to Herbert's pub. They had a drink, doubled back, and pulled in to the car park. Quinn would later make a statement detailing the events of that Thursday night. In it, he admitted to being frightened when it dawned on him that the IRA unit was planning an armed robbery:

> I was shit scared. I knew at this stage that it was an armed robbery that Kevin was planning. After a few minutes, a white car pulled in close to us. Kevin got out and sat in the white car. I could hear them discussing the robbery ... I knew they were senior IRA men. Kevin Walsh called me over to the window of the car and said 'I am expecting a few people here, everything will be alright.'

Nobody connected with Finnegan's had an inkling as to what was happening outside in the public car park. John Quinn recognised one of the men as Pearse McCauley, the Strabane Provo who had escaped from Brixton Prison in England in 1991. In 1993, McCauley had been caught in the Republic with a pistol and twenty rounds of ammunition and sentenced to seven years in Portlaoise, but was released two years later, on 6 November 1995. Quinn turned around and saw a dark Pajero jeep pulling past him into the car park. The driver got out, a tall dark-haired man. He threw something into the ditch, removed his gloves and put them in his pocket. John Quinn heard one of the men introducing the newcomer as Johnny from the midlands. Also present was the OC (Officer Commanding) of the IRA's Southern Command. Originally from west Belfast, he had come south in the 1970s and had settled in south Dublin. By 1996, he had separated from his wife and was living with his girlfriend in a flats complex in Dublin's north inner city.

The OC was the driving force behind the notorious Munster 'fund-raising' unit of the IRA, which had carried out a string of bank robberies during the 1980s and early 1990s, upon which the organisation relied financially. Outside of the North, the south-west was where the IRA's toughest operators were based. Between February and May 1992, a garda search operation in Munster uncovered fifteen IRA arms dumps, which housed an array of weapons, including thousands of rounds of ammunition, sixty-six assault rifles and three RPG7 anti-tank rockets.

The OC was sitting in the white car with the other IRA men with the window open when Quinn heard a row break out. One man, thought to be the OC, said: 'There is to be no ramming, it's too dangerous.' Another argued: 'Everything has been Okayed from the top' which Quinn took to mean the robbery had been sanctioned by the IRA. 'If it has to go that way that's it, or if anything goes wrong you'll find yourself with a bag over your head in Armagh,' said another Provo. Kevin Walsh walked over to John Quinn and said the men wanted him to do 'pilot'. By that stage, the stolen Mitsubishi had arrived in the car park. Walsh asked Quinn to drive in front:

> We went the back roads. Kevin 'The Fox' was driving the Pajero; Pearse McCauley was driving the Mitsubishi. Kevin was driving behind me … He flashed the lights at me … He told me he wanted diesel and I was to get some but I was to lead them to Kevin's father's house first. When we got [there] the gates opened and the Pajero and Mitsubishi went into Walsh's yard and the gates closed again. I continued on.

With the planning over, the OC left the car park and went home to Dublin. Johnny went back to the midlands. John Quinn returned to Faha to fetch a plastic container for the diesel and, from there, went to a garage on the Dock Road in Limerick. He dropped the filled container outside Paddy Walsh's. Kevin Walsh had told Quinn that there would be a bag dropped off for him at a certain passageway and he was to deliver it to Paddy Walsh's house. Quinn found the coloured bag, and when he opened it, he saw it contained ammunition clips for a Kalashnikov AK 47 automatic assault rifle and balaclavas. He was wearing blue gloves, which Kevin Walsh told him to burn. When all that was done, John Quinn went back to his girlfriend's house and went to bed.

Earlier that night, the duty officer in Henry Street Garda Station in Limerick had been rostering armed detectives for security detail the following morning, 7 June. Two runs were down for that Friday morning: one to Newcastle West, the other to Adare, to escort a post office van delivering £81,000. It was a toss of a coin as to which pair of detectives would be assigned to which run. The duty officer marked down Ben O'Sullivan and Jerry McCabe for the Adare run, commencing at 6 a.m.

JERRY MCCABE had been awake from early that morning. He was a tall, fairly good-looking man with dark hair. He was looking for a shirt, one that had been ironed.

'Are there any ready?' he asked his wife, Ann.

'They're all there, Jerry, just look for one.'

By 5.50 a.m., he was ready to leave his house in Avondale Drive in Greystones, an estate on the outskirts of Limerick city. He shouted goodbye to Ann and said he'd be back around ten o'clock for a break. He took with him a cup of tea to drink later, put his standard issue firearm — a .38 Smith and Wesson — into his holster and walked out the door. Detective Garda McCabe was in good spirits as he left for Henry Street that morning. In two weeks' time, he and Ann were due to go on holiday to Spain with another couple. He planned to retire within a year or so and start his own business, installing electrical appliances.

McCabe drove to the station in an old Ford Granada, arriving just after 6 a.m. Detective Garda Ben O'Sullivan was already there, revving the engine. The two were old friends. They had met back in the mid-1960s when they worked in Dundrum in County Tipperary. They were both transferred to Limerick, first to O'Curry Street and then to Henry Street, were promoted to the Special Branch on the same day in November 1972, and covered roughly the same district. They even lived near each other. O'Sullivan, a father of four from Mourneabbey, County Cork, is a jovial, well-built man with a receding hairline. In his younger days O'Sullivan was a prominent rugby player and an expert rower. In 1994, he was awarded the Scott Gold Medal for an act of bravery in disarming a man with a loaded shotgun on the streets of Limerick. Jerry McCabe was from Ballylongford, County Kerry. At fifty-two, he was the same age as Ben O'Sullivan. He had studied at Rockwell College and then went on to University College Dublin to study languages. He dropped out after a year, and in 1964, he joined the gardaí. Three years later, he married Ann Cuniffe, the daughter of a Limerick garda. 'Jerry had a ball for the year he was in UCD but his heart wasn't in it,' his wife recalls.

It was normal for Jerry McCabe and Ben O'Sullivan to team up on security detail. They escorted cash deliveries about once a week, McCabe acting as observer while O'Sullivan drove. When O'Sullivan reported for duty that Friday morning he was told that he and McCabe were on the Adare run, stopping first at Adare and then other post offices along the route. William Jackson was driving the An Post truck. The detectives had signed out an Uzi sub-machine-gun and by half past six were ready to go. They were travelling in an unmarked Special Branch car, a dark blue Ford Mondeo. The truck and the garda car proceeded westward from the General Post Office on Henry Street through Limerick city and on to Adare, a distance of roughly ten miles.

Adare is one of Ireland's prettiest villages; in the summer season it is always packed with tourists. Historic Adare Manor is at one end of a long, main street, which veers to the left near the top of the village. Main Street is where the post office is located and where William Jackson was due to drop off a delivery of cash, cheques and postal orders.

It was roughly 6.55 a.m. when the truck stopped at the post office. The garda car cruised to a halt about six feet behind the truck. Jackson got out and, operating a lift attachment, lowered the lift and opened the rear door. He climbed on the lift, got in the truck and unfastened the harness holding the mail in place. Jerry McCabe and Ben O'Sullivan were sitting in the garda car. O'Sullivan looked in his rear-view mirror and he saw a jeep with a bullbar coming up behind at high speed. There were two men in front with their heads covered. O'Sullivan could see they were driving straight at them.

'Jerry, oh Jesus, Jerry,' he shouted.

The jeep rammed them from behind, square on. With the impact, Ben O'Sullivan's arm snapped and he was pinned to the steering wheel. As this was happening, the Mitsubishi Lancer pulled up alongside the garda car and its left side crashed into the jeep or the garda car. There was one person inside with a balaclava over his head. The gunmen jumped out of the jeep and were now standing on either side of the Mondeo. Two of them took up position in front of the Special Branch car. The two men inside were now completely ringed by five heavily armed IRA men. Neither man had a chance to draw his revolver. Ben O'Sullivan told this author of the sequence of events that ended with the death of his friend, Jerry McCabe:

> The jeep was coming right in on us. They were dressed in green and black army combats. In the background I saw a car, then the bullets, they started ripping me. My arm, whether it snapped from the ramming, I don't know, but I was welded to the steering wheel with the impact. When the shooting started, my shoulder was riddled. They didn't break the window: they shot through it. The first blast I got in the shoulder, the second blew my hands off the steering wheel. Then I saw the blood pouring off my head. I was pinned beneath the dash and the console of the car when the third blast got me on the side of the head. At this stage I was below Jerry. I saw his hands contracting like they were in a spasm. I called him a few times but there was no response. I tried to turn my fingers into Jerry's wrist but there was no pulse.

William Jackson had been unfastening the harness inside the truck when he heard the ramming, quickly followed by heavy blasts of gunfire. The terrified driver jumped from his truck and sat on the footpath facing the masked men, with his hands in the air. When the shooting stopped, three of the men ran towards the silver Mitsubishi. No attempt was made to remove the mail from the van. 'Leave it. Go, go, go!' one of them roared. They were shouting at the top of their voices as all five jumped into the silver car and sped off in the direction of Rathkeale, with Jeremiah Sheehy at the wheel. They left the jeep at the scene. Ben O'Sullivan tried not to lose consciousness; he knew that if he did he would bleed to death: 'I kept trying to keep myself conscious. There were two radios in the car; the second one was wide-ranging. I realised control was calling us but they were calling us on the first radio. I went to pick it up but it fell through my fingers.'

O'Sullivan was riddled: the gunman had fired eleven armour-piercing bullets from the AK 47 into him. 'My whole body was vibrating. I knew there was enormous damage done to my right shoulder,' he said. William Jackson tried to summon help on his cab radio. He ran over to O'Sullivan, who was bleeding profusely. 'Hang in there, Ben, hang in there,' he whispered to the critically wounded man. Jerry McCabe was beside him, slumped over the passenger seat. He was dead. The cup of tea he had brought from his house just an hour earlier was still in a cup-holder below the dashboard.

A local GP, Dr Van Kuyk, arrived at the scene shortly after 7 a.m. and pronounced Jerry McCabe dead. He had been hit by three bullets, one of which had lodged at the back of his throat. He died from haemorrhage, shock and laceration of both lungs. The doctor covered his body with a blanket. Ben O'Sullivan was rushed to Limerick Regional Hospital: 'They were very secretive in the hospital, but I knew, I knew Jerry was dead.'

JOHN QUINN'S girlfriend was awakened at 7.10 that Friday morning by the sound of sirens blazing as they passed her house outside Patrickswell *en route* to Adare. She ushered Quinn to the window to have a look. 'Oh Jesus!' he said. In his statement of 11 June 1996, Quinn said:

> I knew when I heard the sirens, I knew the vehicles I led up to Walsh's and the ammunition I dropped up there were used in a robbery. When I saw the pictures on the television … of the Pajero and the Mitsubishi I knew they were the ones I brought up to Walsh's which were used in the robbery.

At the McCabe home in Greystones, the two youngest children, Stacey and Ross, were upstairs studying. The Leaving and Junior Cert. exams had started. Ann McCabe was expecting her husband to return at 10 a.m. when the doorbell rang. It kept ringing persistently. Ann McCabe was still in her dressing-gown. She looked out the window and saw John Kerin, a detective inspector from Henry Street, on the doorstep with a bangharda. Kerin was white from shock.

'Your name is Ann McCabe? Ann, I have a bit of bad news. Jerry and Ben, they were injured,' he said.

'How bad? Come on in.'

'Ann, Jerry is dead.'

At that point everything went blank, Ann McCabe told this author:

> I started screaming. Stacey and Ross were hysterical. John [their eldest son, also a garda] was stationed in Monaghan; he was on the same shift as Jerry. He had called the station

and asked them 'Was it my Dad?' They said 'Yes'. He rang me and said 'Mam, I'm on my way home.' He was driven down to Limerick and he got sick on the way. I can't describe the next few hours; all my neighbours came down. Jerry's brother, Mike, heard on the news that two guards had been shot in Adare. Mike's wife knew Jerry was on earlies, but at that stage the lines to Henry Street were jammed. And all this time, Jerry was still in the car.

It was three o'clock that afternoon before Jerry McCabe's body was removed from the garda car, placed in a coffin and driven away in a hearse. Exactly thirty minutes earlier, gardaí had found the silver Mitsubishi Lancer, with false Dublin number plates, in an isolated laneway at Liskennett, near Granagh village, a rural area six miles from Adare. In the Lancer, gardaí found a round of Kalashnikov ammunition, the plastic ties that John Quinn had bought for Walsh and a container of petrol. The gang had abandoned the car and switched to another getaway car, the red Nissan Sunny that had been stolen in Thurles. 'We knew within a half an hour who was behind it,' said a senior garda source. Almost immediately after the murder, a team of Limerick detectives had raided the homes of Kevin Walsh, Jeremiah Sheehy, John Quinn and another well-known republican, Michael O'Neill. Detectives from Nenagh had also sped to a house in Puckaun, in Tipperary, where Pearse McCauley had been living. Every one of them was missing.

PATRICK HARTY is a bachelor farmer who runs a ninety-two-acre holding at Clonolea in Toomevara, a scenic village nestled in the foothills of the Silvermine Mountains in County Tipperary. He used to farm cattle, but they got wiped out by TB so he switched to sheep farming. Harty's farm is set back, although visible, from the main Dublin to Limerick road. Sometime during 1993, four men arrived at the farmhouse and asked Harty if he would 'mind a couple of cars'. He agreed to do so, reluctantly. They put two cars into a shed and covered them with bales of straw and hay. Harty knew the first man as 'Rusty' or 'Ginger'. He was Kevin Walsh; another was Michael O'Neill. Of the other men, one was thirty-four and from west Cork, while the other was forty-four and living in Shannon, County Clare. About a week later, some of the men returned to collect the cars. It was night-time. They asked Harty if they could call back the following morning. He reluctantly agreed and they returned around breakfast-time. In a later statement, Harty said he suspected something was up: 'I thought something had happened as they were all very edgy. They had at least one gun, which I saw, they had walkie-talkies and they had a number of bags which looked like money bags. The four of them stayed all day at my place.'

Harty made it clear that he did not wish to become involved in anything dodgy. In late 1994 or early 95, the Clare man stopped by at Harty's house but did not ask for anything. More than a year elapsed before the farmer met any of them again. It was towards the end of May 1996. Kevin Walsh and the Clare man arrived at the farmhouse in a large saloon car. They took out a green bag measuring about eighteen by twelve inches with double handles and a zip down the middle. They put the bag in the shed and Harty locked it with a padlock. Walsh returned a week later, collected the bag and drove off. It was a few days before the Adare shooting.

On the morning of 7 June, Patrick Harty awoke to the news that two gardaí had been shot during an aborted robbery in

Adare. At around 9 a.m., he heard a car pulling into his front yard. It was the getaway car, the stolen Nissan Sunny. Kevin Walsh, Jeremiah Sheehy, Michael O'Neill and the man from Clare got out of the car. Pearse McCauley got out of the boot. Harty immediately thought of the Adare raid and suspected something was afoot. They asked if they could stay for a while. Harty was afraid to refuse. He put on the kettle and stoked up the fire. The five men were tense, but controlled. They were muttering among themselves. Gay Byrne was discussing the Adare shooting on the radio and Harty asked them if they wanted to listen to it. 'Not really,' one said. The men were up and down to the bathroom, washing themselves and looking for towels.

One of the Provos asked Harty to drive him to Puckaun, a village thirteen miles north of Toomevara. He had a Northern accent, which Harty found difficult to understand. He said he was taking some clothes from Harty's farmhouse: petrol blue trousers, a blue baseball cap and black shoes. The farmer realised that he was Pearse McCauley, the Brixton escapee. (Ironically, McCauley had replaced another Provo on the Adare raid who had to cry off over a family bereavement.) McCauley gave Harty directions to his girlfriend's house in Puckaun. Along the way McCauley mentioned something about signing on, which Harty presumed meant signing on the dole.

He let McCauley out on a back road to go the rest of the way by foot. Harty drove on to Nenagh to do some shopping and returned home at 11 a.m. The news came over the car radio that one of the gardaí in Adare had died. Harty was becoming increasingly jittery. When he got back to the farmhouse, the four Provos were still there. He told them he was worried about the car, the Nissan Sunny. 'It's a clean car, don't worry,' said the man from Clare, but he drove it around to the slatted shed anyway. Harty parked his tractor in front of it and went out to test his herd. When he came back in, he spotted a handgun on the surround of the electric fire in his bedroom and a military-style rifle at the foot of the bed. It was an AK 47. Harty told the Provos to get rid of the guns. They asked him to burn some green woollen caps and some socks, which he threw into the range.

'This is a bad business,' the farmer muttered, referring to the murder in Adare. According to Harty's statement of 11 November 1996, they neither admitted nor denied involvement:

> I then left the house … until about 6 p.m. then returned home. I was hoping they would be gone, but when I arrived home the four men were still in my house. I asked if everything was alright. The four of them were in the attic bedroom and one of them said 'We'll be going soon.' After a short time they came down to my bedroom and they huddled around the radio and were listening to it intently. They asked me if I had seen any garda checkpoints. I told them I had not. They asked me to get cigarettes and razors. I told them I'd have difficulty getting the razors as I wear a beard.

Patrick Harty drove to Toomevara village and bought forty Major cigarettes in Kelly's shop. When he returned he found an old electric razor in the house and gave it to them. Kevin Walsh asked Harty for a handsaw to 'cut the stock of a gun'. Chairs had been placed in front of the range with shirts and jeans hanging on the back of them. It appeared to Harty that the clothes had been washed while he was out. The Clare man and Kevin Walsh were still huddled over the radio in Harty's bedroom. Michael

O'Neill and Jeremiah Sheehy were in the attic. The Clare man sent Harty off to Nenagh to buy Ordnance Survey maps of the midlands and Dublin. On his return, the farmer spread the maps on a small table and was making himself scarce when Kevin Walsh called him. 'There's stuff to be burned,' he said. The 'stuff' consisted of dark green boiler suits, more woollen gloves and the timber stock of the gun that had been cut earlier.

When they were finally ready to leave, they asked for a blanket and a holdall, got the car from the slatted shed and left the house, one by one. As he was leaving, Kevin Walsh mentioned the guns in Harty's bedroom and said someone would be along to collect them. Walsh drove the car down the lane, turning left for Toomevara. When they had gone, Harty went upstairs for the guns, wrapped them in plastic bin-liners and tied them with tape. He waited until darkness had fallen, then took them outside to a field and buried them. Then he cleaned the house from top to bottom, erasing any remaining traces of his visitors.

AT 2.48 P.M. on the day of the murder, the IRA issued a statement firmly denying any involvement in the aborted raid or the killing of Detective Jerry McCabe: 'None of our units were in any way involved in this morning's incident in Adare. There was absolutely no IRA involvement — P. O'Neill.' The caller gave the code-word 'Eksund'.[1] The shooting dead of a garda detective had a profound effect on the general public, particularly since the IRA had been on de facto ceasefire since

1 'Eksund' was the recognised IRA code-word at that time: it has since been changed. All IRA statements are signed 'P. O'Neill'.

February 1996.[1] On 28 February, the British and Irish governments had issued a joint communiqué announcing a date for all-party talks on the North. It was 10 June, three days after the killing of Jerry McCabe. The murder in Adare was a public relations disaster for the Provos, coming as it did days before Sinn Féin expected to take its place at the talks. The party was subsequently excluded from the 10 June talks at Stormont because of the IRA's failure to call a renewed ceasefire.

By the time the IRA statement was phoned into RTÉ, the gardaí were already searching for a specific group of fifteen Provos attached to the Munster unit. The unit around Limerick had almost sole responsibility for armed robberies. The aborted robbery bore all the hallmarks of an IRA operation: it was planned with military precision along the lines of previous IRA raids on bank and post offices, and the weapon used — an AK 47 — was used almost exclusively by the IRA. Subsequent ballistics tests on the bullets found at the scene of the killing showed that the Munster unit which had taken £94,900 from a post van on Limerick's Kilmallock Road exactly two years earlier had used the same weapon. Senior gardaí briefed the government on who they suspected was responsible: the Provisional IRA.

The government was slow to attribute blame; with the Stormont talks about to start, the timing was ultra-sensitive. There was a lot of politicking going on. Senior government ministers were playing down newspaper reports that civil servants were instructed to request the gardaí to refrain from publicly blaming the IRA. In an interview on RTÉ on Sunday,

1 On 31 August 1994, the IRA called a ceasefire, which was broken on 9 February 1996 by the Canary Wharf bomb in London. But from February until 15 June 1996, when the IRA bombed Manchester, a de facto ceasefire situation existed. The IRA declared a renewed ceasefire from 20 July 1997.

9 June, the Minister for Health, Michael Noonan, placed some reliance on Friday's IRA statement. These statements had been pretty accurate in the past, he said. Noonan did acknowledge that the *modus operandi* and weapons used suggested the involvement of IRA members, or former members who still had access to this type of weaponry. But he was still not convinced the Provos were behind it: 'That speculation was fairly widespread on Friday and into yesterday but I understand that a number of lines of inquiry are being pursued now and the certainty of the first conclusion is being diluted somewhat.'

In a complete U-turn, on 15 June the IRA issued a second statement admitting that its members killed Detective McCabe. But it said the Adare shootings 'were not and could not have been sanctioned' by the leadership because they were in direct contravention of the IRA's standing orders. (The IRA's General Army Order No. 8 prohibits 'military operations against 26-county forces under any circumstances whatsoever'.) A government spokesman admitted that the latest IRA statement was 'confirmation of what we already knew from the Commissioner'.

BEN O'SULLIVAN spent four days in the intensive care unit of Limerick Regional Hospital before being airlifted to Belfast for specialist treatment. His injuries were horrific and took months to heal: 'I was burning; not only did the bullets go through but the charge did as well.' O'Sullivan's detective duties had included monitoring the movements of known republicans, specifically members of the IRA and INLA. He knew them all well, and they knew him. As mentioned, he had disarmed a man pointing a loaded shotgun at passers-by in Limerick city and was awarded the Scott Gold Medal for bravery in 1994.

One can still see the mark of one of the bullets from Adare at one side of Ben O'Sullivan's forehead. Some of his fingers have been irreparably damaged, but, that apart, his physical wounds have largely healed. The psychological scars will take a lot longer to heal. When talking about 'survivor guilt' the former detective, who retired in 1999, becomes emotionally upset:

> The perception is that if a guard knows a criminal, it can be an advantage to the guard [in relation to police work] but it is also a disadvantage to him in that the criminal knows how that guard is likely to react in a crisis. He knows the way he thinks. If they [McCabe's killers] knew I had disarmed people before, then they might know I would be likely to resist being disarmed myself in Adare. If I thought that then I would be responsible for Jerry's death.

Ben O'Sullivan had no doubt, from early on, who was behind Adare:

> I could have named three of the five. Ordinary criminals do not carry that kind of firepower. Where does an ordinary criminal get an AK 47? They would not do a robbery like that. To see it as it developed, it had to be an organisation. They tried to claim there was only one magazine blast. If that was the case, how would I be able to give the precise sequence of the blasts? The first blast got me in the shoulder, the second blew my hands off the steering wheel and the third got me in the head when I was trapped down between the dash and the console. If there was just the one blast, all the bullets would have been in the one direction.

Ben O'Sullivan was still in Limerick Regional Hospital on Monday, 10 June, when Jerry McCabe was buried. Two local priests stayed with him in the hospital while the state funeral was taking place. Limerick city came to a standstill that day. In the stilled streets, the sound of the marching feet of hundreds of uniformed gardaí was a grim reminder that, in the midst of optimism about the impending Northern talks, peace remained illusory. Government ministers and senior members of the Opposition stood side by side with the Garda Commissioner, Patrick Culligan, and deputy garda commissioners. It was a dignified, sombre and very public affair. State funerals do not allow space for private grief, reflects Ann McCabe:

> When it's a state funeral, everything is taken out of your hands. It's very public. Our private grieving didn't really start for two years after Jerry was killed. Our friends and neighbours and the guards were very good; they kept calling and calling. At the funeral home . . . a reporter from *The Examiner* stayed outside with Ian [the third eldest son]. Mark [the second eldest] was hysterical. That day, Ross stayed in bed all day long with his head under the covers — he was the closest to his father. Stacey stayed in the house. The house was full; Jean Kennedy Smith called to the house and gave me a pair of rosary beads that belonged to her mother, Rose. As the days went on, I don't know exactly when, I became aware of the IRA statement. At first they denied it, then they said it wasn't sanctioned. It wasn't something that was discussed with me because everything was a total blur.

THE HUNT for the killers of Jerry McCabe was a massive operation. About forty-five minutes after the shooting the Air Corps helicopter was on its way from Baldonnel to Limerick. Garda checkpoints were backed up with heavily armed troops from Limerick and Cork. One of the first searches was concentrated in several squares miles of countryside in north Kerry. It turned up nothing. A memo from garda headquarters had been flashed to air and sea ports naming four men wanted in connection with the Adare shooting: Kevin Walsh, Michael O'Neill, Jeremiah Sheehy and the man from Shannon, County Clare. The names of Pearse McCauley and the man from west Cork were later added to the list. The memo said all were still believed to be in the country, and were thought to be armed and dangerous and likely to resist arrest.

At 7.05 on the morning of Sunday, 9 June, gardaí arrested John Quinn at his girlfriend's house near Patrickswell. He made a lengthy statement detailing his own involvement and that of a number of others. That was the first break in the case. Up to that point, the gardaí had never heard of Patrick Harty, the farmer whose house the gang had used as a bolthole. Quinn did not know Harty by name, but he described exactly where his house was. When Quinn was asked to sign he said: 'If I sign that I will be shot.' John Quinn was charged with IRA membership and possession of ammunition at Patrickswell on 6 June. (He later claimed in court that he had been injured while in garda custody. In the course of his detention he had been brought to Limerick Regional Hospital on four occasions and was treated by four different doctors. However, the court found no basis for the allegations. It said that Quinn was treated 'strictly in accordance with the law'.)

At 9.55 p.m. on Sunday, fifteen hours after John Quinn's

arrest, gardaí detained Jeremiah Sheehy in Rathkeale under section 30 of the Offences Against the State Act. They took him first to Henry Street Garda Station and then transferred him to Roxboro Road, where his period of detention was extended. He told the gardaí nothing. Chief Superintendent Ted Murphy rang the Director of Public Prosecutions, Eamonn Barnes, who directed that Sheehy should be released, rearrested under section 21 of the Offences Against the State Act and charged with firearms offences and membership of the IRA.

That Sunday morning, at 8.30, there was a knock on Patrick Harty's door. A man he had never seen before asked: 'Are they here?' Harty thought he was referring to Kevin Walsh and the other Provos. He told him they were gone. When Harty asked the stranger his name he said to call him Mick. 'There's some stuff to be collected,' said the farmer who wanted rid of the guns hidden in the field. Mick said he would ring back on Thursday and they would meet that night. He arrived at Harty's at eight o'clock on Thursday evening and the farmer handed him the guns, one plastic bag and a bucket. That was the last he saw of him.

The following week the gardaí arrested Patrick Harty. He was in way over his head and now he wanted to tell all. What he was able to tell the gardaí enabled them to piece together what had happened on the day of the killing. And more crucially, who was there. From police photographs he identified by name Kevin Walsh, Pearse McCauley, Michael O'Neill, Jeremiah Sheehy, the Clare man and a Limerick Provo as the men who came to his house either before or after the robbery. Harty also told them about the 'hardware' that they had brought into his house on the day of the killing:

I saw at least two, if not three military-style rifles, one sawn-off shotgun single barrel, and one pistol, together with the firearm that they cut the stock off and which they must have taken with them. There was three twelve-bore shotgun cartridges which I threw out the window of my car one day when going to the dump at Ballymackey, Nenagh.

Later, Harty made a signed statement in his solicitor's office in Nenagh and agreed to become a prosecution witness. It was not until they spoke to Harty that the gardaí realised that it was his land that the Munster unit had been using to hide cars and other materials, a fact that Harty admitted. 'All the times we'd passed that house, we never knew,' said a senior security source in Dublin. 'We knew they had to be going somewhere after the jobs, but we never knew this man existed.' On 18 June, Michael O'Neill was arrested and charged in the Special Criminal Court with IRA membership and possession of firearms at Clonolea, Toomevara, on 7 June 1996 and possession of a firearm with intent to endanger life at Adare on the same day.

After her husband's death, Ann McCabe left to go on holiday with friends. It was the Spanish break that she and Jerry had planned months earlier. As the holiday was drawing to a close, she heard on the radio that journalist Veronica Guerin had been shot dead in Dublin. She cut short the holiday and headed home. A family friend, Keith Lancaster, was at Dublin Airport to meet her. As they came through the first-class lounge, the Fianna Fáil leader, Bertie Ahern, and his partner, Celia Larkin, were sitting reading the paper; apart from that it was empty: 'He just looked up at me but neither of them said anything. Only a fortnight before he had attended Jerry's funeral. I felt bad when I thought about it, but that's it. We went straight to the church.'

By early 1997, the gardaí had charged a number of men with IRA membership as part of the Adare investigation. They had found the two IRA men who had stolen the Pajero and the Mitsubishi. One of them was later convicted of IRA membership and unlawful possession of firearms. But there was no sign of the prime suspects. The Cork man's wife is Venezuelan, and gardaí suspected that he managed to leave Ireland and get to Central America shortly after the shooting. They were almost certain the others were still in the country, hiding in safe houses. It was only a matter of time before they were caught.

On 11 May 1997, Pearse McCauley surfaced in County Cavan. A detective inspector from Monaghan spotted him driving a car on the Belturbet to Ballyconnell road. The gardaí chased after him but McCauley managed to escape. Later, he called to the holiday home of an Englishman and asked him for a lift to the Slieve Russell Hotel in Ballyconnell. In the car, McCauley pulled a gun: 'I think you have a problem,' he told the Englishman. 'If the gardaí catch me my friends will kill you.' McCauley threatened the man with kneecapping. When he refused to take him any further, McCauley sped off in the Englishman's car. It was later found abandoned in Sligo.

Two months later, heavily armed gardaí in Dublin and Offaly arrested the OC of the IRA's Southern Command and John Carroll, from Birr in County Offaly. The OC was in bed when they raided his Dublin city-centre flat. Both men were taken to Henry Street Garda Station in Limerick. Carroll was questioned about what had occurred in Finnegan's car park in Annacotty on 6 June 1996.

'My heart wants to tell ye but I have to stay with the advice of my solicitor. Nobody wants to see a guard shot,' Carroll said. (His solicitor had advised him in the normal way to communicate with the gardaí only in the presence of his legal representatives.)

'Did you meet John Quinn there that night?' a detective asked.

No response.

'Reading from John Quinn's statement it would appear you are a very high figure in the IRA.'

'What was said in the [Sunday] Tribune puts me on a pedestal way above what I was.'

'There is no smoke without fire,' the detective responded.

'I have told you I have severed all my connections and I am not saying anymore.'

The day after he was arrested, Carroll gave a signed statement admitting membership of the IRA. He said he 'had been a member for a number of years, but as a result of incidents culminating in Adare on 7 June, had severed all connections with the organisation'. The welfare of his family was what concerned him now. Carroll had agreed to answer questions about the meeting in the car park on the eve of the killing, through his solicitor. He subsequently backtracked on this. John Carroll later pleaded guilty to IRA membership and received five years, suspended. The OC refused to answer questions put to him in custody. But the gardaí felt they had sufficient prima facie evidence to enable them to charge him with membership of an illegal organisation. They released him and sent a file to the Director of Public Prosecutions recommending a charge of IRA membership. The OC promptly went on the run. Gardaí issued a warrant for his arrest, but he is now in Spain where he is running a bar.

That October, the gardaí finally caught up with Pearse McCauley. He had been hiding out at Tully Cross near Renvyle,

County Galway, at the home of an IRA sympathiser. McCauley and his girlfriend, Catherine Fitzgerald, were walking home at 3 a.m. after a night out. They used the beach to avoid being spotted on the road. They were in the middle of a blazing row and McCauley was shouting and roaring when the gardaí pounced. He was still shouting at her while they were putting handcuffs on him. It was Fitzgerald's home address in Puckaun that McCauley had used for signing on while on bail for a previous offence. McCauley was brought to the Special Criminal Court and charged with possession of firearms at Adare on 7 June 1996.

There was still no sign of Kevin Walsh, the Cork man or the man from Clare. Walsh's luck ran out the following March when gardaí made a dawn swoop on a safe house. It was a farm near Mullagh, in County Cavan. Walsh had been there for over a year and a half, since early September 1996. He had dyed his hair black and had begun wearing glasses. He had also obtained a false passport, a Scottish one. Walsh seldom left the house, but when he did, he would jump into a ditch if a car came along. While in Mullagh, he busied himself doing work around the house and garden. He built a brick wall across the garden, a fishpond and a wall across the end of the cowshed.

Walsh also began to speak about what had happened at Adare. He told the farm owner's daughter that 'a car and a jeep load' of Provos were there. One of the guns stuck on automatic and it went off. He said they 'were not supposed to shoot at the guards but the bullets were going everywhere'. Two of the Provos looked into the garda car and saw blood along the front of it. They thought the two gardaí were dead. When they realised what had happened, they aborted the robbery and took off. One of the Provos had vomited after the killing.

Kevin Walsh kept a Kalashnikov rifle with him in Mullagh, along with two loaded magazines taped together with red insulating tape. He also had a handgun. Every time he went out, the handgun went with him. During this period he went back to Limerick twice to see his wife. On one occasion he arrived back at the farmhouse with a harp made by republican prisoners in Portlaoise. When the gardaí raided the farm at 8 a.m. on 10 March 1998, Walsh was in the kitchen. He ran into a bedroom carrying a loaded Marakov pistol with eight rounds of ammunition up the back of his trousers. Another magazine with eight rounds was stuffed into his front pocket. A fully loaded Kalashnikov AK 47 with sixty rounds of ammunition — with the safety lever off — was lying on the floor of the bedroom. They arrested Walsh and immediately began a search of the farmhouse. Initial searches turned up 136 rounds of ammunition, a large quantity of forged driving licences, balaclavas and equipment for monitoring garda frequencies.

The entire family was arrested: four that morning, one later in the day and another in Rathmines in Dublin the following day. All made statements. The man who owned the farm showed gardaí where he had had weapons stored on it. Then he directed them to neighbouring lands where weapons were hidden. The people on whose lands the weapons were stored had no idea what had been buried there. The farmer took the gardaí first to his cooling house in the milking parlour, which had a false ceiling. Hidden above it were six short firearms. 'Kevin Walsh cleaned the guns before I stored them,' he said. Next stop was across the road to a neighbouring farm. There, in a fenced-in haggard, were two plastic barrels containing three heavy bags. When gardaí opened the bags they found an AK 47 and some magazines. The AK was one of twelve dropped there by the IRA's quartermaster general (QMG). He had collected eleven of them shortly after.

The farm owner admitted that the Clare man had also hidden out there for three months, from September to December 1996. The man who drove them there was QMG:

> While [the Clare man] was in my house, he kept a lot to himself. He spoke very seldom about the murder in Adare but I could see that he was deeply troubled by what happened. He told me that Kevin Walsh was very hard to handle ... that what they did in Adare was wrong and that he himself was the most unlikely terrorist in the world ... I am sorry for what I was involved in with that crowd.

The farmer subsequently pleaded guilty to possession of firearms and explosives and was sentenced to four years' imprisonment by the Special Criminal Court. The rest of his family were released without charge.

In an interview with one of the man's sons, the gardaí asked if Walsh had spoken about the killing.

'Did Kevin say where he was sitting in the jeep when it hit the patrol car?'

'He did say, as he was getting out of the jeep that his foot caught in the door.'

'Did he say who fired the shots?'

'All he said was that the jeep crashed into the back of the patrol car ... his foot caught and a gun went off and a detective was shot.'

'Was it Kevin Walsh's gun that went off?'

'He didn't say it was his gun that went off, he said a gun went off.'

'Did Kevin Walsh during his chats with you ever show any

remorse over the killing of Jerry McCabe?'

'He said the job went wrong, that it shouldn't have happened. He said it was an accident and that there was no plan beforehand to kill anyone.'

A second son was then questioned about the Clare man: 'Do you know where he is now?'

'I know he is living in Dublin but I do not know where ... I have the impression he lives somewhere near Rathmines.'

'What did [he] tell you about Adare?'

'He said it was an accident, he seemed more disturbed than Kevin ... he was very distant.'

'Did he tell you anything else?'

'He told me he stayed in Tipperary after the murder.'

'Had [he] any visitors?'

'[QMG] landed one day while [the Clare man] was there. He went and chatted to the two of them and went away again ... he [the Clare man] was sorry for what they had done. He said he didn't fire a weapon. You could see it in him, he was never smiling, he looked fucked.'

On 11 March, gardaí arrested the farmer's daughter in Dublin. She later made two statements relating to Kevin Walsh's time in the farmhouse. On the same day the gardaí missed the Clare man by a whisker. He had arranged to call to the daughter's rented flat in Rathmines, Dublin, that morning. She had been living there while studying at a Dublin college. He had been due to pick up the book of evidence relating to Jeremiah Sheehy's case at 11.30. It was in a blue and white shopping bag on the top shelf of a wardrobe. When the Clare man called, the daughter had already been taken into custody. The flat was empty.

A CHARGE of capital murder had been preferred against Jeremiah Sheehy and Michael O'Neill in June 1997. When Pearse McCauley was captured he too was charged with the capital offence. With Kevin Walsh now in custody, the four co-accused were returned for trial for the murder of Detective Jerry McCabe. John Quinn stood trial on conspiracy to rob, possession of firearms and IRA membership. The five men faced a total of thirty charges. After lengthy adjournments, the trial finally got under way in the Special Criminal Court in January 1999.

Walsh, McCauley, Sheehy and O'Neill appeared in the dock wearing the green ribbon symbol for the release of republican prisoners. Prosecuting counsel Edward Comyn said it was the state's case that neither garda had the opportunity to draw his revolver when the Pajero jeep rammed the garda car. He said the plan was to put the gardaí out of action by close fire from an automatic weapon. Detective McCabe died in a hail of fifteen bullets fired from a single Kalashnikov rifle, but there was no evidence as to who had fired the shots.

Patrick Harty had been due to testify against the accused on day seven of the trial. But when he got into the witness box, he refused to do so. He was clearly afraid.

'Mr Harty, from the book of evidence you have evidence to give of an extremely important nature,' said the presiding judge, Mr Justice Richard Johnson.

'I am sorry,' Harty responded.

There was no evidence that Harty had been got at. His solicitor, Liz McGrath, regretted that her client was unable to give a reason for not testifying. The only hint of possible retaliation should he give evidence was when she referred to Harty as a 'bachelor farmer, with no brothers or sisters and who lives alone at his farm in a secluded spot'. He was sentenced to eighteen months for contempt. It was Paddy Walsh's address that was cited on the firearms charges relating on 6 June, although he himself was not charged. He had made a statement but refused to give evidence when in the witness box and was treated as a hostile witness.

The state's case was now in serious trouble. The murder trial collapsed dramatically on 2 February when the men changed their pleas from not guilty to murder to guilty to manslaughter. Pearse McCauley and Kevin Walsh were each sentenced to fourteen years. Jeremiah Sheehy was jailed for twelve years and Michael O'Neill for eleven. Quinn was sentenced to six years for conspiring to commit robbery at Adare. The judge noted that Sheehy, O'Neill and McCauley had expressed regret for the killing but Walsh had not. McCauley smiled briefly as he was led from the dock; the other four showed no emotion.

On the day of sentencing, Patrick Harty, who had spent a fortnight in jail, was brought back to the Special Criminal Court where Liz McGrath was pleading for mercy on his behalf: 'Mr Harty is sitting in jail, not a happy man, and not just because of his term of imprisonment.' She had reason to believe he had been subjected to 'pressure' that had led him to fear for his own safety and that of others. 'The only reason he has found himself before this court is due to his obliging nature and sense of loyalty to the past which was clearly manipulated.' He was a deeply troubled man and had told her: 'Liz, I fell at Beecher's Brook.' The court relented and freed Harty after he had purged his contempt. As Harty left the dock, Mr Justice Richard Johnson warned him to take his solicitor's advice in future.

Ann McCabe and Ben O'Sullivan left the court, chased by the waiting media. How did they feel, now that it was all over, the reporters wanted to know. 'No comment, really, no comment,' they responded apologetically. Two years on, Ann McCabe recalls the day the murder charge was reduced to manslaughter:

> We were taken downstairs and told it's going to be manslaughter. We were disappointed but we were told 'You're looking at at least twenty years.' Ben was on his way up, John Kerin was there. Then we went up to the courtroom and sat down. Stacey was with me, and all Jerry's family. Their supporters were sitting on the other side. When I heard one of them, I think it was Walsh but I'm not sure, saying he had no remorse it was the final nail in the coffin. We felt dreadful when the sentences were announced. I thought it was totally wrong. Jerry's father died two years ago. Towards the end he'd say 'Where's Jerry?' and then he'd remember and his eyes would fill up. He never got over Jerry's death.

According to the family who had provided the safe house, neither Kevin Walsh nor the Clare man had intended to kill anyone that morning. The gun had gone off accidentally. If that is true, then the manslaughter verdict reflects the non-intentional killing. But forensic evidence on the trajectory of the bullets showed that they went in all directions. This suggests that more than one blast had been fired. And from Ben O'Sullivan's account, the ferocity of the attack strongly suggests that the killer, or killers, intended to take both men out — O'Sullivan took eleven bullets. The fact that the object was to rob makes their actions on that morning even more inexplicable. According to John Quinn's statement, the IRA had sanctioned the robbery — it was no solo run. The OC of the IRA's Southern

Command who was outside Finnegan's car park for the last-minute planning would have had every authority to sanction it. What was not sanctioned was the shooting of a garda, which is clear both from the order forbidding the ramming and from the IRA statement of 15 June. It is highly possible that one of the gunmen lost control and shot to kill, and in killing Jerry McCabe and wounding Ben O'Sullivan, damaged many lives, including his own. And they got no money. Five years later, Ben O'Sullivan still wonders about the motive behind the killing of his partner:

> I haven't the answer to that. They obviously thought there was a reason, but I don't know. They will have to live with it, but Jerry can't live with it. We had talked a lot about retiring; we didn't have a black and white plan but we talked about it. There's no doubt but we'd have had a joint retirement party. My retirement party, well it made it an awful lot harder for everyone. Losing Jerry … it's like a sheep without a shepherd. Trying to adjust, going back to work was a big step in the right direction. My family, they've learned to live with it. I bought my daughter a horse; I've tried to divert my grief into something positive. I had to get away from Adare in order to get back to Adare, to try to come to terms with what happened. I can still hear the guns rattling.

Since their conviction, a row has raged over whether or not the McCabe killers qualify for early release under the Good Friday Agreement. Sinn Féin and the government are totally at odds on the matter. Sinn Féin is pressing for their release: the Minister for Justice, John O'Donoghue, has assured Ann

McCabe they will serve their full sentences:

> I have every confidence that they will not let them out; I'm
> hanging on to the guarantee I got. There was a meeting in
> 1999 between O'Donoghue, his secretary, Ben and myself.
> When they left I was with O'Donoghue on my own. I told
> him I'd have the whole country behind me. We all voted
> for the Good Friday Agreement, but isn't it ironic, Jerry
> used to often say 'We'll never see peace in my lifetime.' If
> they were going to be released, I'd have to make my
> feelings known; what trust would you have in the
> government after that? Hate is not a word I like to use; it
> eats you up. I do feel bitter when I see them getting all
> those concessions though. You know, Jerry wouldn't be a
> hero for anyone; he valued his life too much. But he had
> no choice whether he lived or died. They didn't give him a
> chance, or Ben.

Since her husband's death Ann McCabe has suffered from
bouts of depression and enormous weight loss. She is also aware
that the prisoner release row is a stumbling block in the peace
process:

> I know Jerry is a stumbling block. I know it. But I can't
> accept that the men who killed him are covered — I will
> not accept it. I was in Dundalk for the Clinton visit and I
> saw Jean Kennedy Smith with Gerry Adams and Martin
> McGuinness and the whole entourage. Jean is a very good
> friend and she asked me afterwards why I didn't come over.
> 'Not with the company you were in, Jean,' I said to her,
> 'not for peace, not ever.' You never adjust to what

happened, you just learn to live with it. You miss your friend, your husband, the father of your children; you miss every single thing. There were days I just sat there, watching the video of Jerry's funeral until a friend took it from me. I do suffer from depression; it directly stems from Jerry's death. Jerry was the kind who would never let you sleep on an argument: I'd be the one to have a puss. It's lonely now. I don't mind my own company but you can have too much time on your own and it is lonely.

The McCabe prisoners are serving the remainder of their sentences in Castlerea's low-security prison. Because he was on bail until his conviction, John Quinn's sentence runs only from the date of sentencing. With remission, he will be released in 2003. Walsh, McCauley, Sheehy and O'Neill will be free men by, at latest, 2008 with remission.[1] None of those who made statements implicating the suspect from Cork are prepared to give evidence against him. In 1997–8 he was working with a non-governmental aid agency in Central America, part-funded by the Irish government on a renewed contract. After contacts with the gardaí, the agency ended its association with him. The man from Clare has not been seen or heard of since 11 March 1998. He is still on the run.

1   In July 2001, John Quinn and Michael O'Neill were given leave by the High Court to seek orders allowing for their release under the terms of the Good Friday Agreement. The case is listed for hearing in late 2001.

13

Garda Sergeant
Andrew Callanan

A picture taken in 1989 shows Sergeant Andy Callanan in full uniform sitting in front of a plaque erected in memory of Garda Patrick Reynolds in Tallaght Garda Station. The plaque hung on the back wall of the old public office facing the large reception area. The office had a wooden counter facing the main door, seating on the right and double doors leading to a corridor along the main building at the back. On one side of the counter was a glass-panelled door behind which was a small office to accommodate a small number of gardaí. Tallaght Garda Station was built in 1988 at a time when the force was trying to improve relations between the gardaí and the public. New reception areas were designed to be less daunting and allow easier communication than the old stations with their bleak public offices. The overall result was a softening of reception areas and a more amenable environment for both the public and the gardaí.

In July 1999, Andy Callanan had clocked up seventeen years' service in the force. He had spent all but six months of it at

Tallaght, where he was the sergeant-in-charge. He was a tall, broad-chested man, with a slightly receding hairline and a smiling face. Sergeant Callanan was married and had three young children, including two-year-old twins. On 20 July 1999, he reported for the night shift at 10 p.m. It was to be his last week at the station: the following week he was due to leave Tallaght to train gardaí in the force's new computer database system, PULSE, at garda headquarters. The night shift runs from ten o'clock until six the following morning. Shortly after 4 a.m., Andy Callanan was getting the night's documents in order before finishing his shift and driving home to Bray, in County Wicklow.

It was around that time that a man walked into the public office. He was carrying a sword, two canisters of petrol and two Japanese flares. Garda John Malone was on duty at the public desk. He was in the small, partitioned office when he heard a noise coming from the main reception area and went out to see what was up. He saw the man place a can of petrol on top of the counter. 'You have two minutes to evacuate the building,' he warned. 'What?' gasped Malone. One side of the plastic container had been cut. Malone watched in horror as noxious fumes began escaping and liquid seeped onto the counter and dripped onto the tiled floor. The detective ran back behind the partition for Sergeant Callanan, screaming that someone was setting fire to the station. As he did so, the man broke one of the red cylindrical objects in his hand, set it alight, and then began to ignite the second one. Bright orange flames shot up from the top of the Japanese flares as the man stood holding them aloft, one in each hand. Callanan, who had rushed to get a fire extinguisher, came through the double doors at the back of the public office into the main reception area. Malone and another garda stood in the doorway holding the double doors open. 'What are you at? What are you at?' Callanan asked repeatedly.

The arsonist was now holding the flares shoulder high. As the sergeant pressed the lever of the extinguisher, the man's arm and the flare moved downwards towards the petrol-drenched floor. It ignited the petrol. Flames shot up, some of which caught hold of the arsonist's clothes and he started to burn. Callanan began spraying him with foam when there was a sudden flash and a loud bang as the petrol exploded, engulfing the public area in flames. One of the gardaí, who had been propping the door open with his foot, was blown out of the doorway by the blast. The force of the explosion threw him towards the corridor at the back of the building.

Andy Callanan took the full force of the blast. Engulfed in a ball of flames, he was thrown against the wall and lay against it, burning. John Malone tried to get back into the reception area to save his colleague's life, but the flames were too intense and he was driven back by the burst of heat. He ran out the back of the building and as he did so, spotted a white Ford Sierra driving away from the station. He made a mental note of part of the car registration number and ran back to the scene of the blast. The station was now in total chaos. Gardaí in the main body of the station knew that Sergeant Callanan was trapped in the inferno in the public area. 'Where's Andy?' Malone asked another officer.

On his hands and knees, Malone again tried to push the double door dividing the corridor from the reception area. It did not open freely because of the burst of heat. He managed to prise it open with his hands and as he put his arm in, through the thick smoke and blackness, he could feel something on the ground. He thought it might be tiles curled up from the heat that were blocking the door. Malone was hoping that what he was feeling was not his colleague, Andy Callanan. Eventually, he got the right-hand door to open and he saw Sergeant Callanan. He was lying with his legs draped across the doors. Malone tried to pull the injured man to safety by the ankles but the sergeant's injuries were too severe. His uniform had been burnt off his body. A female garda, who had previously trained as a nurse, arrived at the scene and searched for a pulse. She could find none. Turning to Malone she said, 'He is gone.'

Sergeant Callanan's injuries were horrific. He was rushed to hospital in a squad car but it was too late. He was pronounced dead at around 6 a.m., the time he should have been leaving the station and heading home. He was thirty-seven years old.

FROM THE car registration numbers that John Malone had managed to commit to memory, detectives had little trouble in tracing the white Ford Sierra. By 5.30 a.m. they had a name and address. It had been registered to a man named Christopher Byrne. They called to his home shortly before 6 a.m. Byrne told detectives that he no longer owned the Sierra; it now belonged to a man called Daniel O'Toole, a thirty-six-year-old security guard. Originally from Cashel Avenue, Crumlin, in south Dublin, O'Toole was living in west Tallaght in July 1999. As soon as the gardaí left, Byrne rang O'Toole and asked him what was up. O'Toole said he would talk to him later. Thirty minutes later, he rang Byrne. 'What's going on?' asked Byrne. He told O'Toole that he had heard about an incident involving a white Sierra. 'Was it yourself?' he asked. O'Toole said he would talk later. He had to go to hospital for treatment for burns.

Shortly after he put the phone down on Byrne, the gardaí arrested O'Toole at his house in Donomore Crescent. They took him to St James's Hospital for treatment. His burns were such that he required a number of skin grafts. As soon as he was well enough to leave hospital, Daniel O'Toole was charged with the manslaughter of Sergeant Andy Callanan. He applied for bail in Kilmainham District Court, but the gardaí opposed the application because of the seriousness of the charge, the nature of the evidence against him and the likelihood that he would abscond if, as predicted, more serious charges followed. Detective Inspector Martin McLaughlin, in opposing bail, conceded, however, that there was no suggestion that the accused would interfere with witnesses and that he had surrendered himself peacefully to gardaí hours after Sergeant Callanan's death. O'Toole was subsequently granted bail by Ms Justice Catherine McGuinness in the High Court under certain conditions: that he would live with his father at Cashel Avenue and sign on twice daily at Crumlin Garda Station. Turning to the gardaí, the judge said that, from their point of view, it was difficult for them not to object to bail, as they had lost 'a valued and valuable colleague'.

Daniel O'Toole had served in the Irish army from December 1980 to May 1982 but had been discharged for being below the required physical standard. He had no history of trouble with the gardaí until the summer of 1998, when his wife, Bernadette, made certain allegations against him relating to a family member. She sought a barring order, which was granted in the District Court in October 1998. He was now out of the family home and having difficulty getting access to his children. Some of his friends and his former employer were aware of his marital difficulties, as were the gardaí who were now investigating Bernadette O'Toole's allegations. She and her three children moved to Enniscorthy, County Wexford. Her husband moved back into the family home in Tallaght.

Daniel O'Toole was subsequently rearraigned and charged with the murder of Sergeant Andy Callanan contrary to section 3.[1] The trial opened in the Central Criminal Court on Wednesday, 13 June 2001, before a jury of seven women and five men. It was the first trial for the murder of an on-duty garda to be heard before a jury since January 1972, when Joe Dillon and Seán Morrissey were tried for the murder of Garda Richard Fallon. (Jury trials for subversive offences were abolished and replaced with the non-jury Special Criminal Court at the end of 1972.) O'Toole denied that on 21 July 1999 at Tallaght Garda Station he murdered Sergeant Andrew Callanan, who was acting in the course of his duties.

While pleading not guilty to murder, O'Toole admitted manslaughter, a plea that the state refused to accept. If O'Toole were found guilty of the murder of a garda he would be given an automatic forty-year prison sentence without remission. A simple charge of murder was also put to the accused, as an alternative charge to that of murder contrary to section 3. He denied the simple murder charge, and also a further charge of arson at Tallaght Garda Station on the same date.

Each day of the trial, the accused hobbled into Court 2 at the Four Courts on crutches and sat to the left of the trial judge, Mr Justice Paul Carney. O'Toole had put on a lot of weight since 1999. For most of the time, he sat hunched over the bench, taking notes and barely glancing at witnesses as they passed him on the way into the witness box. Sitting a few feet away and directly in front of the judge was Yvonne Callanan, the victim's widow.

1   The term capital murder was abolished by the Criminal Justice Act 1990. This Act created a separate offence of murder contrary to section 3 of the Act. The penalty for the murder of a garda or a prison officer is now forty years' imprisonment without remission.

The jury sat through two weeks of evidence, some of it harrowing. The witness testimony cannot be reported for legal reasons. By the close of the trial, the jury was down to eleven members, one female juror having been discharged early on in the trial. In his closing speech, prosecution counsel Peter Charleton put it to the jurors that the central issue for them to consider was whether or not Daniel O'Toole had intended to kill or cause serious injury when he set fire to Tallaght Garda Station that night. 'The intention has to coincide with the act and that's really what this case is about,' he said. In his summing up, defence counsel George Birmingham argued that the intention of the accused was not to kill or cause injury. He put it to the jury that Daniel O'Toole had intended to commit suicide on the night in question.

The jury retired on the afternoon of Wednesday 27 June, but by 6 p.m. they had not reached a verdict. They were sent to a hotel for the night. When the jury resumed their deliberations the following morning, they asked Mr Justice Carney for clarification on the meaning of 'intent'. The best example, said the judge, was from the judgment of a former Supreme Court Justice, Brian Walsh, in the 1977 Supreme Court case of *DPP* v *Murray*, when he said: 'To intend to murder or cause serious injury to a civic guard in the course of his duties is to have in mind a fixed purpose to reach the desired objective. Therefore the state of mind of the accused person must be not only that he foresaw but also willed the possible consequences of his conduct.' The ruling further stated that the mind of the accused could not have intent unless he or she also had foresight. The use of the terms 'capital' and 'simple' murder was shorthand only, and they were not legal terms, Carney added. The press, he said, was 'having difficulty coming up with snappy headlines' and had begun using the terms in reports, thereby forcing counsel and himself to follow suit.

It was clear that the jurors were having difficulty reaching a verdict. Just before lunchtime on Thursday, the jury returned. They were asked if they had reached a verdict on any of the counts on which a majority of ten to one agreed. There was just one, the arson charge, on which all eleven jurors voted to convict. On the murder charges, they were hopelessly deadlocked. Mr Justice Carney sighed. 'The consequences of having a retrial in this case are appalling, truly appalling.' There was a widow and a family to consider, and 'no doubt every single member of Tallaght Garda Station had been affected by this case,' he said. The accused man had also been through a stressful time. This case, mused the judge, 'would take a year to get back on the rails'. He urged the jury to 'go to lunch and have another stab at it'. No matter how long they deliberated, the jury would not be able to reach a verdict, the forewoman said.

After lunch, Mr Justice Carney asked them if they had reached a verdict. The reply was no. Garda colleagues of Sergeant Callanan were stunned. The judge said it was 'unfortunate' and a 'matter of tragedy' that the jury could not return a verdict. He discharged the jury and ordered a retrial. It was at that point that Daniel O'Toole would be sentenced for arson, said Mr Justice Carney. Prosecuting counsel Peter Charleton rose to his feet in protest, and there followed an acrimonious exchange between him and the trial judge. Charleton wanted O'Toole sentenced there and then on the arson conviction. It was 'part of the bigger picture and I'm putting it back to the retrial,' responded Mr Justice Carney. The accused came to the court on bail and he would leave on the same status, he told Charleton. With respect, countered the prosecuting counsel, the accused came to court an innocent man but was now a convicted one, and therefore had no entitlement to bail. The judge sat back in his chair and glowered. 'I'm putting it back to the retrial,' he repeated. Andy Callanan's widow, Yvonne, left the court in tears. Daniel O'Toole walked out of Court 2 on bail.

Mr Justice Carney subsequently reversed his decision after O'Toole asked to be taken into custody. On Friday, 13 July 2001, Daniel O'Toole was sentenced to fifteen years for arson. The retrial on the murder charge is expected to be heard in 2002.

Epilogue

Since the founding of the Garda Síochána in 1922, thirty officers have been killed in the line of duty. Most were murdered, although, in a few cases, the killing was downgraded to manslaughter. Sixteen gardaí were killed between 1922 and October 1942, when Garda George Mordant was shot dead in Dublin while trying to arrest a wanted man. From then, not a single officer was killed in the course of duty until twenty-eight years later, when, in April 1970, Garda Richard Fallon was gunned down. He was the first of fourteen gardaí to be killed during the Northern conflict that erupted in 1969 and overshadowed the island for three decades. All but two of the killings, those of Sergeant Patrick McLaughlin and Sergeant Andy Callanan, were carried out by republican paramilitaries or others with a political agenda. Eight of these twelve killings happened during or as a result of bank or post office robberies, and four of the gardaí were armed at the time they were shot down. The IRA carried out six of the killings (plus the killing of Private Patrick Kelly), while the INLA, Saor Éire or a loose band of radical left-wingers were responsible for the remainder.

In much the same period north of the border — 1969 to 1998 — 302 RUC officers were murdered. The vast majority of these were killed by republican paramilitaries, although, ironically, the first RUC victim, Victor Arbuckle (1969, Shankill), and the last, Frank O'Reilly (1998, Portadown), were murdered by loyalists. The crucial difference is that while RUC officers were deemed 'official targets' by republican paramilitaries, the IRA's standing orders forbid the killing of a member of the Southern security forces. However, while General Army Order No. 8 prohibits 'military operations against 26-county forces under any circumstances whatsoever', there is no order forbidding the use of territory south of the border for the benefit of the armed struggle in the North. On the contrary, the five border counties, from Donegal in the north-west across to Louth in the north-east, are included in the IRA's Northern Command and, as such, are part of the 'war zone'.

A recurring theme over the past three decades has been the question of whether or not the gardaí should be armed. Almost without exception, this debate has accompanied every killing of a garda since that of Garda Fallon. The fact that the RUC — an armed force — has a casualty rate twenty-two times higher than the Garda Síochána would seem to validate the argument against arming the gardaí, apart from the specialist detective units. While a number of RUC deaths were prevented by virtue of the officers being armed, in the vast majority of cases, it made no difference.

From its foundation, the Garda Síochána was designed to be 'absolutely unarmed' and was to depend for success on 'moral, rather than physical factors'. For almost fifty years the Southern police force had the luxury of carrying out its duties in a relatively controllable and crime-free environment. But times have changed. The emergence of organised crime in the 1980s and early 1990s, combined with the sudden increase of paramilitary activity from 1969 onwards, tested the gardaí like never before. The response to these new challenges was sporadic, knee-jerk reactions that were, for the most part, politically inspired gestures designed primarily to assuage the public outrage that followed each killing of a garda. The gardaí themselves were divided on the issue of arming the force, with most officers firmly on the side of retaining the Garda Síochána's status as an unarmed police force.

Up until 1978, very few gardaí were either armed or trained in the use of firearms. That year, detectives were balloted on whether or not they wished to be issued with firearms. Most voted no. In the wake of the murders of Detective John Morley and Garda Henry Byrne in 1980, that verdict was reversed, with 239 in favour and 89 against. So, by their own initiative, detectives were issued with Smith and Wesson .38 revolvers. The first move towards increasing the number of armed officers was the establishment in 1978 of the divisional Security Task Force, a specialised fully mobile unit that later became the Special Task Force. Originally comprising just forty officers, this unit had increased to 200 by 1983. As a direct result, the number of bank robberies decreased as criminals turned to 'softer' targets, mainly post offices, which had not the same level of armed protection. The Security Task Force developed gradually into a specialised counter-strike unit that has, over time, evolved into the heavily armed Emergency Response Unit.

The use of the death penalty as a deterrent has been another feature of the debate that has accompanied the killing of each garda over the past thirty years. In 1964, capital murder was created as a separate offence from that of 'ordinary' murder. The death penalty, no longer imposed for the murder of civilians, was retained where the victim was a garda or prison officer killed in the course of duty. The feeling among the general public was that where there existed a largely unarmed police force, society had to be seen to stand behind it. Over the years, capital punishment became increasingly unacceptable to the extent that a significant jail sentence was seen as an appropriate deterrent to capital murder.

The Criminal Justice Act 1990 finally abolished capital punishment in statute law, although it remained in the Constitution until June 2001 when it was removed after a referendum. The penalty for the murder of a garda is now forty years' imprisonment without remission. The reality is somewhat different. Of the fourteen people convicted of the murder of a garda since 1976, ten have been released and only four remain in jail. Of the ten released, four were set free in 1998 under the terms of the Good Friday Agreement. The four men still incarcerated are non-aligned prisoners and are therefore not covered by the agreement.

The disparity of time served and the criteria under which the convicted men have been released are, in some cases, remarkable. The killers of Sergeant Pat McLaughlin — Joseph Greene and Thomas McCool — served less than eleven years in jail, even though Greene was sentenced to life for non-capital murder. This killing stood apart from all of the others in that McLaughlin was deliberately targeted. He was murdered precisely *because* he was a garda (although in McCool's case the charge was downgraded to one of manslaughter). McLaughlin's killers did not belong to any political group, which seems to suggest that it is the *motive* behind the killing, rather than the act itself, which is the crucial factor in determining how long the convicted person will spend behind bars. Although not covered by the Good Friday Agreement, the killers of Sergeant Paddy Morrissey and Garda Henry Byrne had some connection with paramilitary or left-wing groups and are still in jail.

A number of the bereaved families, particularly the Fallon, Clerkin and Donegan families, are very unhappy with the reluctance of the Department of Justice and the garda authorities to provide even the most rudimentary information surrounding the killing of their loved ones. By pure coincidence, between 2000 and 2001, these three families contacted the authorities seeking answers to questions that have dogged them for up to thirty-one years. They each met a stone wall. While it is fair to point out that there is not a police force in the democratic world that would open its files to scrutiny on security grounds, it is hard to see why the garda authorities would continually refuse answers to the most basic questions put to them by the families of Sam Donegan and Michael Clerkin.

The Fallon case is in a different category because of the political connotations that surround it, even thirty years on. While the British government is making a (belated) effort to confront some of the mistakes of the past, through the Bloody Sunday and other inquiries, the Irish authorities appear incapable, or unwilling, to follow suit. Des O'Malley, then a rising star in Fianna Fáil and later leader of the Progressive Democrats, took over as Minister for Justice shortly after Dick Fallon was murdered and is therefore in a position to know what was happening behind the scenes at that time. When the Fallon family contacted him in 2001, O'Malley advised them to wait until the documents dealing with Frank Keane's extradition are released to the National Archives. Most of the answers are in those papers, he said. However, these documents are not being released under the thirty-year rule. The Department of Justice has classified them as 'security' documents. They are being kept secret. Dick Fallon's youngest son, Finian, views the department's refusal to address issues surrounding his father's murder as unacceptable, given the length of time that had elapsed since his father's death and demands by the Irish government that Britain investigate controversial incidents that happened in Northern Ireland. Apparently, the Irish government thinks it quite acceptable to stand at the border and lecture the British on the virtues of 'coming clean'. It is quite another matter for the Irish government to do the same.